How Not to Reinvent the Wheelbarrow

HERB MILLER

HOw NOt to Reinvent the Wheel (barrow)

Basic Biblical Christianity

ABINGDON PRESS
Nashville

HOW NOT TO REINVENT THE WHEELBARROW

Copyright © 1990 by Abingdon Press

This book is printed on acid-free paper.

Library of Congress Cataloging-in-Publication Data

MILLER, HERB.

How not to reinvent the wheelbarrow: basic biblical christianity / Herb Miller.

p. cm.

ISBN 0-687-17684-0 (alk. paper)

1. Theology, Doctrinal—Popular works. I. Title.

BT77.M535   1990

230—dc20

89-29955
CIP

Unless otherwise marked, Scripture quotations are from the Revised Standard Version of the Bible, copyrighted 1946, 1952, © 1971, 1973. Used by permission.

All Scripture quotations marked KJB are from the King James Version of the Bible.

Poem excerpt on p. 125 from William Carlos Williams, *Collected Poems, 1939—1961*, Vol. II. Copyright 1955 by William Carlos Williams. Reprinted by permission of New Directions Publishing Corporation.

Manufactured in the United States of America

*To a bright new light in our family,
grandaughter Jill Nichole Wright.*

CONTENTS

INTRODUCTION

he visiting speaker at a church dinner in North Carolina noticed the giant plastic trash can near the kitchen door. As people dumped their used paper plates and cups into it, the big letters stamped on the side caught his attention: "Property of the San Diego Zoo."

When the visitor asked the pastor about this unusual sign, he jokingly replied, "If you were here on Sunday morning, you would understand."

"Oh, I see," said the visitor, falling in with the levity, "I just had not seen that particular religious symbol before."

That plastic garbage can describes what happened to many religious beliefs during the past few decades. Christians have for centuries defined the basic concepts of their faith in generally agreed upon ways. Concepts like sin, salvation, and God had standard meanings. Now, many people have redefined these concepts in such irregular ways that the concepts could accurately carry the label, "Property of the San Diego Zoo."

What caused these distortions of centuries-old Christian beliefs? Disconnection! The great truths of Christianity are biblically based. Disconnect them from their biblical rootage, and they begin mutating into bizarre shapes.

Why have these distortions become so prevalent now, rather than earlier in history? Among the several causes, three are especially potent. *First, a democratic society that encourages individual opinion naturally produces some extreme beliefs.* Three city children were watching a calf in their grandfather's pasture. One child thought it was a boy calf; another said it was a girl calf. They resolved the agreement by deciding to vote on it. The basic concepts that make up Christian faith are not ideas floating in a vacuum, subject to confirmation by popular vote or a Gallup poll. A Christian is someone who, through the power of a continuing spiritual relationship with Jesus Christ, seeks to do and say what Jesus said and did. The only place we can go for documentation of what Jesus said and did is the New Testament. Authentic Christian beliefs are therefore biblically based. Making them totally personal-opinion based is like voting on the sex of a calf—subject to a wide margin of error. That is, however, more likely to happen in a society committed to freedom of thought.

A second reason for disconnection from the Bible and subsequent distortion of basic Christian beliefs: *the manner by which beliefs are now transmitted from mind to mind.* In the first Christian centuries, beliefs were transmitted in story form—memorized stories of what Jesus said and did, passed on from one generation to another. By the beginning of the third century, however, beliefs were transmitted in creed form—like The Apostles Creed:

> I believe in God the Father Almighty, maker of heaven and earth; and in Jesus Christ his only Son our Lord: who was conceived by the Holy Spirit, born of the Virgin Mary, suffered under Pontius Pilate, was crucified, dead, and buried; the third day he rose from the dead; he ascended into heaven, and sitteth at the right hand of God the Father Almighty; from thence he shall come to judge the quick and the dead. I believe in the Holy Spirit, the holy catholic Church, the communion of saints, the forgiveness of sins, the resurrection of the body, and the life everlasting. Amen.

With the sixteenth-century Protestant Reformation and the Gutenberg printing press, ideas and beliefs began to be transmitted by words on paper—in the case of Christian beliefs, the words of the Bible translated into the language of each country. With the arrival of the television set in homes during the 1950s, beliefs and ideas began being transmitted in oral and visual images—huge volumes of images, images of every kind. Since that time, people have been raised on a cafeteria line of thirty-minute situation comedies that present hundreds of alternative lifestyles and viewpoints. Evening newscasts try to tell both sides of every story. Small wonder that we started thinking that the great ideas of our

Christian faith are matters of subjective opinion rather than objective truth!

A third reason for disconnection from the Bible and subsequent distortion of basic Christian concepts: *the increasing tendency to believe that taking the right actions is more important than believing the right ideas.* A prominent speaker often shocks conservative congregations by saying, "I really don't care what you believe. Tell me what you do." His important point is a great attention getter, especially among the type of Christians who take overmuch pride in the purity of their doctrinal thinking. Yet, the statement, if taken literally and to its logical extremes, contains a major fallacy. What we do grows out of what we believe. If our actions fall short, the cause of that failure often lies in faulty beliefs. The rubber of Christianity hits the road in actions, but the energy for those actions begins in the gas tank of belief. Faulty fuel produces slow or no motion.

Christians have stopped burning people at the stake for having unchristian beliefs. The opposite extreme, however, is almost as bad—thinking that what people believe does not matter. Beliefs are not harmless. What the mind believes, the body eventually does. Beliefs that stray off course are like rockets that lose their intended trajectory. They can hurt the people in them and the people on whom they fall.

How can we correct these distortions? By examining contemporary religious beliefs to see if they are biblically based. Each of these chapters, therefore, communicates one of the basic truths of Christianity. It then contrasts that basic truth with ideas that many people think of as Christian but are actually distortions of that biblical truth. This is not, however, a "systematic theology" book—not in the classical sense of that term. This is a practical book about Christian faith for laypersons. Systematic theology books have value, but they are written primarily for use by theology professors who talk mostly with each other about theoretical concepts. This book is written for average laypersons who talk with each other about the convictions that determine the way they live their lives.

The book is divided into four parts: "The Hub"—the central

core of truth in Christianity, "The Spokes"—the various means by which people connect with the central truths of Christianity, "The Wheel"—the ways in which individual personality is strengthened by connecting with the central truths of Christianity, "The Wheelbarrow"—the ways in which people who connect with the central truths of Christianity change the world.

When Methodists from ninety countries gathered for their fifteenth World Methodist Conference, Joe Hale, general secretary of the council, said to them, "Many Methodists, as well as friends in other Christian communions, would welcome from this gathering a call—a call to a clearer understanding of and a deeper commitment to what is most basic in Christian thought and experience."[1]

This book has precisely that objective. We do not need to reinvent the wheelbarrow of Christianity. The blueprints are in the Bible. What we do need is clarity about what those blueprints say. Without that clarity, we tend to build distorted models that do not roll and cannot move us and our world toward better days.

PART I

THE HUB

*CENTRAL BELIEFS
OF BIBLICAL CHRISTIANITY*

CHAPTER 1

SLIVERS AND SUBSTITUTES

Early one morning a visiting professor was pouring a cup of coffee in the student lounge of a seminary. Beside the coffee a box of pastries awaited the arrival of hungry ministerial students. On the wall behind the rolls and donuts, a hand-lettered sign caught the professor's attention.

COFFEE 20¢
ROLLS 50¢
DONUTS 35¢

PLEASE DO NOT CUT "SLIVERS" OFF A DONUT.
IF YOU CUT A ROLL IN HALF, PAY FOR THAT HALF.

God is the central belief of biblical Christianity. Distortions of that central hub take two forms: slivers and substitutes. In the "sliver distortion," people cut a small slice off of the biblical description of God and operate as if that one part of God's personality were the whole thing. Example: The person who sees God as a rule-enforcing judge and believes this is the sum total of God's nature. Another example: The person who sees God as a loving, forgiving parent and believes this is the sum total of God's nature. In the "substitute distortion" of God, people substitute a completely different god for the one the Bible describes. Examples: devil worship and witchcraft.

The destructiveness of these slivers and substitute distortions make it essential for us to have an accurate understanding of God. A woman said that a friend of hers can talk forever to anyone about anything. She once answered the phone and talked for thirty minutes with a wrong number. Some people talk with the wrong

God for a lifetime. They substitute "being religious" for relating to the God of biblical Christianity. Their wrong number in religion inevitably stunts their lives, personalities, and potentials.

A little girl had been working intently with pencil and paper for a long time. "What are you drawing?" her mother asked.

"A picture of God," the little girl said.

"But no one knows what God looks like," the mother said gently, not wanting to dampen her daughter's artistic enthusiasm.

"They will now!" the little girl said.

The following list is not a naive attempt to provide a complete picture of God. No one has a camera that big. Space does not permit a discussion of all the adjectives, nouns, and verbs the biblical record uses to describe God. Nor can we quote all of the biblical verses that illustrate each attribute of God's nature. The list does, however, furnish a view of the hub belief of biblical Christianity. Reviewing these can help us to identify many of our slivers and substitutes.

Singular

"The Lord our God, the Lord is one" (Mark 12:29).

Distortions: Hinduism, a religion born in India, teaches a multiplicity of gods. Pantheism, the formal name for that belief, says that trees and rocks can have gods in them.

That plural concept often arrives on other shores wearing a different guise. Horoscopes and some of the other occult practices are the most obvious contemporary examples of making God plural—but not the most dangerous. Highly educated people are too smart to think trees have gods in them, but they repeatedly make gods out of individuals like Hitler. And they repeatedly make new gods out of ideologies like socialism or fascism. Whenever Jim Jones or any other religious guru calls for total allegiance to himself or his goals, we are witnessing a westernized form of pantheism—the idea of more than one God.

Creator

"In the beginning God created the heavens and the earth" (Gen. 1:1).

Distortions: Countless variations of the idea that people and the world they live in came about by accident.

The earth is approximately 93,000,000 miles from the sun, just right to sustain life. The earth is tilted on its axis twenty-three-and-one-half degrees, insuring the seasonal changes without which much of the globe would be a desert. The air we breath is 21 percent oxygen and 78 percent nitrogen, perfect for supporting life. An ozone layer in the upper atmosphere shelters the planet from the sun's deadly ultraviolet rays. None of these facts proves that an intelligent force organized things that way. But these and countless other scientific observations point like a thousand fingers toward the creator God of biblical Christianity.

Living

"And Joshua said to the people of Israel, 'Hereby you shall know that the living God is among you' " (Josh. 3:10).

Distortions: The "God is dead" theology of the 1960s. Communism. Atheism, which says God does not exist. Agnosticism, which says that if God exists it doesn't matter. The several types of humanism, some of which proclaim God exists in the form of a nice, helpful idea and some of which see him as an early ancestor who got us started. All the types of humanism (which the Supreme Court in "Torcaso v. Watkins" declared as one of the several non-theistic religions in the United States) see societal progress and personal development as do-it-ourselves projects.

Present

"Whither shall I go from thy Spirit? Or whither shall I flee from thy presence?" (Ps. 139:7).

Distortions: The deists (who numbered Ben Franklin and Thomas Jefferson among their ranks) saw God as an absentee landlord or "first cause." They did not see God as nonexistent or dead. Rather, they seemed to think of him as a once creative genius who is either asleep, in a coma, on vacation, or a tired worker who took early retirement.

We hear someone articulate some form of that distortion every day. A person with AIDS in a prison hospital, who was being interviewed by a TV news reporter, said, "If there is a God, I hope he hears me." In biblical Christianity, God always hears us, because he is always present. Each square inch of human skin has 1,300 pain-sensing nerve endings. When a nurse gives us a penicillin shot, we get a sudden reminder that the brain is attached to each of these 1,300 nerve endings. God is related to us. God is not just living; he is *present—everywhere*. When a sparrow falls, he knows. "In him we live and move and have our being" (Acts 17:28).

Spirit

"God is spirit, and those who worship him must worship in spirit and truth" (John 4:24).

Distortions: The Mormon religion contains many fine people, but in the Mormon faith God is not Spirit; he is an exalted man with a physical body. Because of this and many other views that differ greatly from those found in the Bible, Mormonism has never been classified as a denomination of Christianity. It is as much a separate world religion as is the Moslem faith or the Hebrew faith.

Christianity also contains many opportunities for distorting this aspect of God's nature. Religious ritual without a spiritual focusing of the heart is not worship of the God who Jesus says is Spirit. The giving of financial gifts to the church—or the sacrificial offering of time and energy—does not by itself connect us with the God of biblical Christianity.

Person

"Therefore I tell you, do not be anxious about your life, what you shall eat or what you shall drink, nor about your body, what you shall put on. . . . Look at the birds of the air . . . your heavenly Father feeds them. Are you not of more value than they?" (Matthew 6:25-26).

Distortions: Jesus describes God as a loving, caring person who gives each of us the personal attention of a good father. In contrast, some theologians describe God as a generalized "ground of being" that permeates the universe like a vague mist. The technical name for this view is Panentheism, which says that God is everywhere in general but no place in particular. In this view of God, all people and things exist like patterns in a piece of cloth that is God. God is in all and all is in God. The several types of thinking in the New Age Movement distort the God of biblical Christianity in this way. People who hold these views are not atheists; they do believe in something. But because they have stopped seeing God as a person, they have begun to think like the woman who, when asked if she were religious, said, "Yes, I believe in everything a little bit."

The recent furor surrounding attempts to eliminate sexism from biblical descriptions of God are another distortion of God as person. According to Genesis, God created us in his image as both male and female (Genesis 1:27; 5:1-2). But Jesus does not describe God as an androgynous half-male, half-female person. Arguments in that direction are a sincere effort to correct an injurious inequality with regard to the role of women in our society. Unfortunately, this method of trying to correct that problem introduces a distortion regarding the God of biblical Christianity. God is person. Trying to make him both sexes at once distorts that by making him a mist. Changes in contemporary society may account for part of this trend. Scholars who study and teach world religions point out that for thousands of years, in every part of the world, agricultural-based societies tend to see their gods as female. Hunting-based societies tend to see their gods as male. Some of these world religion experts are wondering whether the important contributions of the nature-environmentalist-ecology movement influenced the current desire of many to see God the father as God the mother.

Loving

"He who does not love does not know God; for God is love" (1 John 4:8).

Distortions: Jesus says God is a person, but not just any kind of person. God is a loving, good parent type of person, always willing to forgive our intentional and unintentional mistakes. When someone says after losing a loved one, "God has done this to me because of the sins I have committed," their pain (and sometimes their feelings of guilt) are distorting the God of biblical Christianity.

Knowable

"Draw near to God and he will draw near to you" (James 4:08).

Distortions: Jesus went beyond saying that God is a loving, spirit person. God is not a distant relative who cannot afford a telephone or is never available for an appointment. God is knowable, and we know him through prayer (Matt. 6:6). When people say that knowing God in a personal way or that knowing God's will for your life is impossible, they are distorting biblical Christianity. Jesus says that God is available for consultation. He not only knows us; we can know him. If we meet with him in prayer, we find out what he thinks.

An old story has the rabbi of Kotzk asking a group of learned persons, "Where does God dwell?"

They laughed and said, "That's easy. Is it not written, 'The whole world is full of God's glory'?"

But the rabbi was taking a different angle. "God dwells wherever human beings let God in." That is very near to what Jesus said. God is not just a good idea; God is knowable.

Relationship Seeking

"You shall love the Lord your God with all your heart, and with all your soul, and with all your mind" (Matt. 22:37).

Distortions: Persons are God's highest and most valued form of creation. God loves each of us and wants the same kind of trusting love from us that the best of loving parents receive from their children. This means that God wants more from us than wisdom, more than morality, more than service to our neighbors, more than regular church attendance, and more than the belief that he exists. When we place one of these high ideals on the altar of our mind—instead of a personal relationship with God—we are doing a

Nicodemus distortion. Nicodemus was intelligent, learned, and religious. Yet, he knew he had not connected with the God Jesus described. Hungry Nicodemus is the picture of many religious persons. He knew he wanted what Jesus had, but he was not quite sure how to get it. Jesus told Nicodemus that he needed to start over—be born again into a childlike, trusting relationship with God.

Jesus reserved his most sarcastic criticisms for the Pharisees, who had developed the Nicodemus distortion to a high religious science of rules and regulations. The prostitutes have a better chance of getting into the kingdom of God than you do, Jesus told them (Matt. 21:31). An evangelist used to conclude every sermon with this statement: "God loves you. Now, you love him back." That is the essence of what Jesus told Nicodemus and what Jesus said was the first and greatest commandment: "You shall love the Lord your God with all your heart, and with all your soul, and with all your mind" (Matt. 22:37).

Provider

"The Lord is my shepherd, I shall not want; he makes me lie down in green pastures" (Ps. 23:1-2).

Jesus instructed us not to be anxious about anything—food, clothing, or tomorrow: God will provide for us (Matt. 6:31-34). That aspect of God's nature takes two forms: One might be called a *general providence*, in which God makes provision for everyone in equal ways. For example: "He makes his sun rise on the evil and on the good, and sends rain on the just and on the unjust" (Matt. 5:45). The other form might be called *special providence*, in which God gives special gifts of guidance and help to those who develop a trusting relationship with him. Example: "If you then, who are evil, know how to give good gifts to your children, how much more will your Father who is in heaven give good things to those who ask him" (Matt. 7:11)!

Distortions: The modern form of this distortion of God's nature is usually called humanism. Since this term itself has been distorted in the media, and in the minds of some people, perhaps we should call it "selfism" or "me-ism." In this view, God leaves us on our own to work things out. Like a benevolent grandfather, he sits on the front porch rocking while we struggle. He loves us and wants us to succeed, but he does not lift a finger to help us.

The various types of "selfism" are extremely hard to identify because they come disguised in admirable human traits. Rational thinking, for example, is something we all need, but if we see rational thinking as our *only* form of assistance, it becomes a "selfism" quite different from biblical Christianity. Hard work is essential to success in most endeavors, but if we see hard work as the *only* road to success, it becomes "selfism." Psychological self-help and the various types of therapies obtained from professionals are valuable, but if we see these as the *only* ways to attain maturity in personality, they become "selfism." Positive thinking is a wonderful trait, but if it is the *only* thing we count on to solve our problems, it becomes "selfism."

The Christian form of this "selfism distortion" is good works. In this view, church people must work harder to change the world for the better—without expecting God to lend a hand along the way. In this theology, we do not enter the kingdom of God. The kingdom of God is inside of us, and no place else. "God helps those who help themselves" is the favorite comment of those who buy into this form of "selfism." What they usually mean is that God helps *only* those people who help themselves. In the Bible, God helped many persons who neither worked for his help nor deserved it.

Carried to extremes, each of the wonderful traits we have noted above—rational thinking, hard work, self-help, psychological therapy, positive thinking, and good works—becomes a functional atheism that believes nothing happens unless we make it happen. The phrase on the back of a tee shirt a traveler saw on the East Coast—"Made in My Own Image"—aptly describes this distortion of biblical Christianity. In this form of atheism, we do not build a golden calf to worship; we bronze ourselves and our own thinking into a golden calf. Christianity says we cannot work things out alone, apart from God's shepherding guidance, and that to think we can is to become our own god.

All Knowing

"**Nothing is covered up that will not be revealed, or hidden that will not be known**" (Luke 12:2).

Distortions: Jesus says that God sees our deepest motives as well as our exterior behavior and holds us accountable for both. We distort this teaching by performing religious rituals or making large donations, to compensate for failure to form a genuine relationship with God and meet the requirements of God's righteousness in our lives. God knows, not just what we put in the offering plate, but also what we hold in our minds as we make that offering. God knows, not just that we go to church, but also what motivates us to be there. The same is true for all that we do and everywhere that we go.

All Powerful

"**I am God Almighty**" (Gen. 17:1)

Distortions: Jesus says that nothing lies outside God's sphere of authority and influence: He can move mountains, heal the sick, and stop storms. A contemporary distortion of this teaching says that God not only does not help us; he cannot help us. He has set the universe and history in motion, but like the official who fires the starting gun at a race, he cannot influence its outcome. This distortion invalidates prayer in general and declares null and void Jesus' line in the Lord's Prayer suggesting that we pray for our daily bread.

Eternal

"**From everlasting to everlasting thou art God**" (Ps. 90:2).

Distortions: God was active in biblical times, but he no longer interacts with people in personal ways.

Judge

"**There is one lawgiver and judge, he who is able to save and to destroy**" (James 4:12).

Distortions: God is so loving and kind that he looks the other way with regard to all human indiscretions. Rather than acting like a good father, he acts like a doting, irresponsible parent who smiles when his children play in the street and manufacture TNT with their toy chemistry sets.

Singular, but Plural

Richard Cardinal Cushing once told this experience from his days as a young priest. He was administering the last rites to an aged derelict who had collapsed in the street. "Do you believe in the Father, the Son, and the Holy Ghost?" Father Cushing asked. The derelict replied, "I'm dying and you ask me riddles?"[1] Many people feel that way about the concept of the Trinity. The mathematics just do not work. One plus one plus one does not equal one.

Nowhere in the New Testament do we find the word "Trinity" or any speculative doctrine about the idea. We do, however, find these statements of Jesus and Paul that point in that direction. Jesus puts it this way: "Go therefore and make disciples of all nations, baptizing them in the name of the Father, and of the Son, and of the Holy Spirit" (Matt. 28:19).

Paul puts it this way: "The grace of the Lord Jesus Christ and the love of God and the fellowship of the Holy Spirit be with you all" (II Cor. 13:14). How can we understand this unusual math? By seeing these three as three different ways in which we experience God. He acted in creating the world and us. He communicated himself in Jesus Christ so that we could fully understand him. His Spirit is externally present to guide and nurture us.

Distortions: Every modern distortion of the Trinity excludes one or more of the three parts of God's personality. Some see God as an absent lawgiver, impossible to comprehend and relate to. Others see God as a good teacher—Jesus Christ—but nothing more. Still others are determined to totally capture God in the emotional feelings that they are sure come from his Spirit to their spirit. All of these are experiences of God, but none of these, alone, is the God of biblical Christianity.

Indescribable

"Not that any one has seen the Father except him who is from God; he has seen the Father" (John 6:46).

The early Church fathers wisely concluded that the only way you can ultimately describe God is by agreeing on what God is not. The mystery of God is beyond any human adjectives or description— because God is not human. He is person, but that does not totally define him. God is person on a plane of reality unlike any we have experienced. We must, therefore, describe God in the same way that an ant describes an elephant—from a very limited perspective. We can see some of God at the point where God connects with our plane of experience. But no one can fully explain God. To do that, we would have to be God.

Distortions: People who say with absolute certainty that they know what God is like and what he wants for the world, the people in it, their church, and themselves personally. We can know a great deal about what a spouse or parent is and thinks, but we can never know them totally. In order to do that, we would need to do more than know a spouse or parent; we would have to be that spouse or parent. The same holds true for our understanding of God.

Jesus

"He who has seen me has seen the Father; how can you say, 'Show us the Father'? Do you not believe that I am in the Father and the Father in me?" (John 14:9-10).

Jesus is a definition and description of God. How do we know God exists? Because Jesus gave us his photograph. How can we know what God is like? Because Jesus told us. How do we know that we can relate to God personally? Because Jesus said we could. Many contemporary copy machines produce a sheet that is identical to the original. In the pages of the Old Testament, we see the outline of God. Through the life of Jesus, we see a perfect copy.

Discovery Questions for Group Study

1. Does the Bible report other attributes of God that are not on this list?

2. Ask everyone in the group to take turns sharing the attributes on this list that are especially meaningful to them. Ask those who are willing to do so to share experiences or ideas which make that attribute meaningful to them.

3. Are there any attributes on this list that you think do not belong here?

4. Are there other contemporary distortions of biblical truth about God that are not noted?

5. Which of the distortions do you think are most common in our community? Our denomination?

CHAPTER 2

THE PERFECT COPY

A business consultant says the world now changes so rapidly that management is like a baseball game with crazy rules: Both the ball and the bases are in motion. When the batter hits the ball, the defending players pick up the base bags and move them. The batters never know in advance where they need to run.

Contemporary thinking regarding Jesus Christ follows a similar pattern. Biblical Christianity says, "He is the image of the invisible God" (Colossians 1:15). Early Church councils like the one at Nicea in 325 A.D. set that conviction into creeds that people could memorize. Missionaries carried that message over the edge of the known world to Ireland and everywhere as the circle of Christianity expanded rapidly. Now, however, distortions of that central belief about Jesus Christ have blurred his identity. Some say Jesus was a good copy but not a perfect copy. Others say he was one of several copies. Still others, like the producers of a controversial movie, say he was an imperfect copy.

For those who try to communicate Christian faith to non-Christians, the ball has always been in motion. Because society changes, thought patterns of those with whom they try to communicate keep changing. Now, however, the bases are also moving. As a young theology student said to a denominational leader, "Many people with whom I speak are sure about one thing: they cannot speak surely about the old doctrines anymore." *Biblical Christianity is Jesus Christ-centered.* But much contemporary thinking depicts a Christ far different from the one in the Bible.

Space does not permit a listing of all the phrases the Bible uses to define and describe Jesus Christ. Then, too, since Jesus is identical with God, repeating the descriptive words from the last chapter would be redundant. We will therefore concentrate on those attributes of God which were seen more clearly when he appeared in Jesus, the Christ. Nor does space permit a listing of all the ways that people distort these attributes. But perhaps these samples can help us to recognize other moving bases when we see them.

Fully God

"I and the Father are one" (John 10:30).

Distortions: Islam teaches that Jesus "was only a messenger of Allah"[1] who did not achieve the greatness of Muhammad. New Age thinkers take a similar view. They see Jesus as one of many "channels" who give us a glimpse of the past. They say he achieved, through many reincarnations, a level of purity available to all of us.

The most common form this heresy of "Jesus as a great teacher" takes among church people is a denial of the virgin birth (Matt. 1:23). Usually based on an unwillingness to believe that reality can take any form beyond that which we can explain with present human knowledge, this distortion denies the divinity of Jesus by saying that a virgin birth is impossible. New scientific evidence indicates that this impossibility may have been overstated. Genetic scientists have discovered that "parthenogenic birth" (conception without male fertilization) happens occasionally in animals and fowls. Scientists suspect that this "miracle" is produced by some kind of virus and are trying to figure it out. The phenomenon is studied among turkeys because it happens so frequently there. Such births are always male—never female. Always extremely strong birds, they have the best possible genetic combination of the mother's traits. This does not mean that the birth of Christ came from a virus or that Jesus was a turkey. It does, however, mean that some forms of reality are beyond our current logical explanation. If a virus can cause conception, perhaps God, acting through the Holy Spirit, can cause conception, too.

The second most common form that this heresy of "Jesus as a great teacher" takes among church people is the denial of Jesus' resurrection from death. "I don't have to believe in the resurrection in order to believe in Jesus," is how many people put it. This harmless-sounding statement masks a deep distortion: It makes Jesus a hero, a great prophet, a martyr to the exemplary cause of self-giving love, and eliminates the God part of his personality.

The miracles of the virgin birth and a literal resurrection are never the real issues in these discussions. They are the surface objections from a much deeper matter. The big question is whether we believe Jesus was, in fact, God. If we do, these and all Jesus' other miracles make sense. If we do not believe Jesus was God, they are irrational impossibilities.

Athanasius, an early theologian, said that when a spring feeds a stream, it is not the stream, yet the water is identical. In the same way, biblical Christianity says that God is in Christ without separation. A contemporary pastor says that we do not call the sun and its rays two different lights. The sun and the way it shows itself are one, just as God and Jesus Christ are one.[2] Both are saying what the Bible says: "He who has seen me has seen the Father" (John 14:9).

Fully Human

"Christ Jesus, who, though he was in the form of God . . . emptied himself, taking the form of a servant, being born in the likeness of men" (Phil. 2:5-7).

Distortions: In the late first century, Docetism, taught by Marcian and a group called the Gnostics, said that Jesus only appeared to be a man. In the late fourth century, Apollinarius taught that Jesus did not have a human spirit. Just as the Council of Nicea had settled the divinity of Jesus in 325 A.D., the Council of Constantinople in 381 A.D. said Jesus was fully human. This and two other church councils—Ephesus in 431 A.D. and Calcedon in 451 A.D.—clarified and affirmed this aspect of authentic Christian Faith. They did so, not on the basis of popular vote but on the basis of what the apostles had taught and passed on in the New Testament writings. They realized that if Jesus can be anything or everything, he will eventually become nothing.

Because our minds cannot logically explain how God can be a person like us, various forms of Docetism and Apollinarianism keep reappearing. Just as some people think Jesus was not God, others think God rented Jesus' body for thirty-three years but never actually bought it. This idea, when carried to its logical conclusion, means Jesus did not actually suffer in the way we would suffer; he just floated through Gethsemane and the cross like a sightseer. According to the biblical record, Jesus suffered everything we suffer except sin. Only in that one respect did his being God make him different from us. Even there, we see "one who in every respect has been tempted as we are, yet without sin" (Heb. 4:15).

When Neil Armstrong climbed down the ladder of the lunar module Eagle on July 20, 1969, he put his feet on another world. But that was not as dramatic as what happened almost 2,000 years earlier. God, in a way beyond human explanation, came to this world and stayed thirty-three years as "God with us" (Matt. 1:23).

Truth Giver

"I am . . . the truth" (John 14:6).

The Old Testament says that we get truth from the Bible: "Thy word is a lamp to my feet and a light to my path" (Ps. 119:105). The New Testament says that we get truth from the mind of Christ: "I am the light of the world; he who follows me will not walk in darkness" (John 8:12). For Christians, Jesus is the living Bible. We read the written Bible to find out what he said.

Distortions: We get the truth only by rational thinking, what we experience personally in daily life, our emotional feelings—"Does it feel right?"—the traditions of our denomination, what the pastor tells us, prayer, or a "spiritual high" experience.

The distortions we find hardest to recognize come from the layers of our own religious culture. In order to bring the truth of God to our minds, Jesus must walk through the maze of ideas that the people in the community where we grew up transmitted about him. But he does make it through this maze. He always comes. He stands at the door and knocks, waiting for us to let him in. That miracle is in many ways greater than Jesus walking on water. Jesus walks on culture and walks on our weak, ineffective ways of transmitting him, and gets home to our hearts anyway.

A teenager watching the beginning of the film *The Ten Commandments* on television saw the credits listing Charlton Heston in the lead role and said, "Charlton Heston. He reminds me of what I wish I was." Jesus does that for each of us. Because he is fully human, he reminds us of what we wish we were like. He is the truth—not just the truth in general, but the specific truth about us, and our potential.

Guide

"Follow me" (Matt. 4:19).

Distortions: We should get our guidance from the set of moral principles passed on by our community to each generation, and from the good example of Jesus' life.

The Apostles' Creed is true to biblical Christianity when it emphasizes that Jesus is not just Savior but Lord. When we make Jesus the Lord of our life, he gives us a guidance that is much more powerful than following rules, codes, religious prescriptions, or the example of his life. Biblical Christianity does not mean that we know exactly what to do in all future situations; it means we know the best of all possible mentors.

The week after Easter, a six-year-old boy was watching his mother tie grapevines to the arbor posts in the backyard. When he asked why, she explained that this would cause the tiny branches to grow in the right direction. He studied the process thoughtfully and said, "Just like Jesus. They nailed him up and now we know which way to go."[3] The transforming relationship of vine to branches: That is what Jesus meant when he said, "Follow me." That is what Paul meant when he said, "Jesus is Lord" (Rom. 10:9).

Savior

"And you shall call his name Jesus, for he will save his people from their sins" (Matthew 1:21).

Jesus is the Greek form of the Hebrew word *Yeshua*, which means "deliverer" or "Jehovah saves!" or "God is salvation." The word *savior* can be understood only by understanding two other biblical words: *sin* and *sins*. Sin is the attitude or condition of self-centeredness that keeps us separated from a relationship with God. Sins are the various ways that this self-centeredness is lived out in human behavior.

From what does Jesus save us? A life of self-centered living, disconnected from the relationship with God that gives us wholeness, meaning, and hope. This salvation from sin (self-centeredness) makes possible salvation from various *sins* that derive from it—sins like anxiety, bad habits, and immorality. How does this work? We can explain that about as well as we can explain how gravity or electricity works. But we can observe that it does work. Belief in Jesus can save people from their sin and their sins.

Distortions: We can save ourselves from self-centeredness by doing good deeds, following good rules, thinking intelligently, giving money to good causes, or living by religious rules. This is like expecting a life preserver to save someone whose plane crashes into the Pacific. The life preserver helps. It holds us on top of the water, but someone still has to come and save us. As a do-it-yourself project, extracting yourself from the middle of the Pacific is not a real option.

The Old Testament Hebrews understood that self-salvation does not work. They knew that we have to reach out beyond ourselves to find new life; reaching inside is not enough. They, therefore, set up systems like burnt offerings at the temple, which assisted people in reaching out. Annual rituals like the Day of Atonement (tenth day of the seventh month) taught people to reach out. Recognizing the limitations in these impersonal methods, they looked for a "Messiah" or "anointed one of God" who would bring at some future time a more complete salvation from self-centeredness.

Towering over New York Harbor is a giant statue that has symbolized salvation for generations of immigrants fleeing every kind of oppression. Within every heart is a "yearning to breathe free" and be all that we can be. Paul is referring to this kind of freedom when he tells us that Jesus saves.

Redeemer

"For the Son of man also came not to be served but to serve, and to give his life as a ransom for many" (Mark 10:45).

When someone is saved from something, someone else has to pay. To save people from illiteracy, a teacher must sacrifice time to prepare a lesson. To save people from drowning, a lifeboat has to go out. To save people who are lost in the wilderness, a search plane must leave the airfield. That is what the cross is all about. It breaks through the walls of our predisposition toward the sin of self-centeredness, gets our attention, and connects us with the reality of God.

Distortions: All the ways we pretend that we are self-sufficient and need no one to help us find wholeness in personality, meaning in living, and hope for the future.

After Abraham Lincoln was assassinated, a funeral procession was carrying his body through the streets of Washington. In the masses that gathered to pay tribute were many blacks who owed their personal freedom to Lincoln's leadership. As the casket passed by a street corner, a mother lifted her tiny daughter above her head so she could see. "Take a long look," she said. "That man died for you."[4] That is what Christians mean when they say Jesus is their redeemer. The cross is God's way of paying the price to reach out and form a positive relationship that saves each of us from our self-centeredness.

Life Giver

"I am the bread of life" (John 6:35).

This bread takes two general forms—bread here and bread hereafter.

Bread Here. Jesus says that those who build their life on his words are building their house on a rock, and those who do not are building on sand (Matt. 7:24-27). He says that those carrying wearisome burdens will find rest in him (Matt. 11:28), and that he is the good shepherd (John 10:11). Paul puts it this way: "And you he made alive, when you were dead through your trespasses and sins" (Eph. 2:1). When we relate to Christ, we are fed by a protein that lets us achieve all the potential of which we are capable. One of the worst business decisions of history was the day William Orton, president of Western Union Telegraph Company, passed up the chance to purchase for $100,000 all patents relating to Alexander Graham Bell's telephone. The value of these patents shortly soared into the billions, and they were soon considered the most valuable the United States Patent Office ever issued. When we pass up a relationship with Jesus Christ, we make an even worse judgment: We pass up the patent rights to eternal life.

Bread Hereafter. "He who believes in me, though he die, yet shall he live, and whoever lives and believes in me shall never die" (John 11:25-26). Jesus said that the reality we experience beyond death is different from, but not less real, than the reality we know now: "In my Father's house are many rooms" (John 14:2). He says that the quality of our relationship with God here influences the quality of our life there. A Scottish preacher says that when he was a prisoner of war in Germany during World War II, early one morning someone shook him awake. The word had come through the underground from the BBC. It was June 1944. The Normandy invasion had succeeded. It would be almost a year before the prisoners in this camp were liberated. No one knew when that would happen. Yet, they ran out of their barracks and rolled on the ground with joy. After the news of that day, life would never go back to the way it had been. Jesus brings that kind of news to human existence.

Church Builder

"I will build my church and the powers of death shall not prevail against it" (Matt. 16:18).

Jesus seems to have operated on the principle that it is better to train twelve people than to try to do the work of twelve. He did not stop with just giving a message. He built a vehicle to carry the message across the world and across the centuries.

Distortions: A wealthy suitor gave his soon-to-be-bride a beautiful gift. "My, what a lovely jewelry case," she said.

"Go on and open it," he said. "The real gift is on the inside." When she unlatched the lid, a diamond necklace sparkled up at her.

In every generation, the institutional church, with all its beauty, pageantry, traditions, beliefs, and good works, so easily becomes the gift to those who love it—while the real gift is undiscovered. "The medium," as Marshall McLuhan said "is the message." In biblical Christianity, the medium is Jesus Christ. If we make something else the medium, like the organized Church, people get that message and miss the real message.

There is, however, an opposite and equally dangerous distortion. In the anti-institutional 1960s, many Christians began to say, "up with Christ and down with the Church." That attempt to correct the idolatry of jewel cases can be fatal if carried to extremes. If Jesus had not needed the Church, why did he bother to call the twelve? Christians will always experience creative tension between Christ and the Church. Making a church (or a denomination) more important than Christ is religious idolatry of the worse sort. But attempting to connect people to Christ without connecting them together as a group is an equally flawed procedure, based on an inadequate perception of human nature. We need both the necklace and the jewel case.

Returning

"This Jesus, who was taken up from you into heaven, will come in the same way as you saw him go into heaven" (Acts 1:11).

Distortions: Saying that Jesus' return has already happened, through the Holy Spirit. Acts 1:1-8 refutes this view. Second, thinking that we know when Jesus will return is a distortion. Mark 13:32 refutes that view. Another distortion is saying that Jesus' return will involve no judgment of wrongdoers. This is refuted in Matthew 24:30-31 and I Thessalonians 1:7-10. A final distortion is saying or thinking that Jesus' return will never happen. Matthew 24:30-31 refutes this view.

C.H. Spurgeon, the great preacher of another era, may have said it best: "I do not know the future, and I shall not pretend to know. But I do preach this, because I know it, that *Christ will come*, for He says so in a hundred passages."[5]

Present in Spirit

"I am with you always, to the close of the age" (Matt. 28:20). **Distortion:** The belief that Jesus lived only thirty-three years.

During the last stages of the war in the Pacific, General Douglas MacArthur returned to the Philippines with enough troops to recapture the islands he had lost to the Japanese in 1942. The Manilla government expressed its appreciation by directing its armies to call out MacArthur's name at every parade roll call. One officer in each company answered, "Present in spirit."[6] Something similar, but much better, happened to the disciples after Jesus' resurrection. He came back in the form of the Holy Spirit.

Discovery Questions for Group Study

1. Does the Bible report other attributes of Jesus Christ that are not on this list?

2. Ask everyone in the group to take turns sharing the attributes on this list that are especially meaningful to them. Ask those who are willing to share experiences or ideas which make that attribute meaningful to them.

3. Are there other contemporary distortions of biblical truth (heresies) about Jesus Christ that were not noted?

4. Which of the distortions do you think are most common in our community? Our denomination?

5. The fundamental work of Jesus as expressed in the Gospel of John is to "reveal God." In what ways is that similar to what churches should be doing today? Different? Can you think of some ways in which churches may be substituting (perhaps without knowing it) some other secondary goals in the place of that primary purpose of Jesus' life?

6. Can you think of illustrations for one or more of the various types of distortions listed in the truth-giver section of this chapter?

CHAPTER 3

GOD'S MICROWAVE

A corporate executive from a town north of Dallas picked up a visiting company official at the Dallas-Fort Worth airport. Heading back home, he got confused in the maze of roads east of the airport near the Texas Stadium. In the spaghetti mix of freeways, he lost all sense of direction in territory with which he thought he was familiar.

Christians often find themselves in a similar situation when they try to explain the third aspect of God's personality—the Holy Spirit. A little girl asked her father,"What is the Holy Ghost?"

The father replied, "That is a word from 1611 A.D., which means spirit. Ghost meant spirit back when the King James Version of the Bible was published."

"The Holy Spirit is a feeling," the little girl's mother added.

"Oh, I see," the little girl said. "You mean like Santa Claus."

Anyone who picks up a Bible can see that *biblical Christianity is Holy Spirit-centered*. The term appears ninety-one times in scripture. Yet, in the contemporary tangle of opinions, how can we begin to find our way home to an accurate understanding of the Holy Spirit? By remembering three facts: First, the Holy Spirit is spirit—both invisible and capable of being everywhere at once, like radio waves. Second, the Holy Spirit is holy—possesses the qualities of God. Third, the Holy Spirit is God—the third way that we can experience the reality of God. Paul speaks interchangeably of the Spirit of God, the Spirit of Christ, and the indwelling Christ (Rom. 8:9-10).

Part of our confusion about the Holy Spirit surely comes from the fact that the most frequently quoted verse on this subject is in the Pentecost report, fifty days after Jesus' final appearance to the

Apostles: "And they were all filled with the Holy Spirit and began to speak in other tongues, as the Spirit gave them utterance" (Acts 2:4). Because that remarkable story sticks in our mind, we easily forget that the Holy Spirit is God and that we find him mentioned in countless other ways all through the Bible. The Holy Spirit is present in the creation account (Gen. 1:2), as the inspirer of prophets (I Sam. 10:10), in Jesus' conception (Luke 1:35), at Jesus' baptism (Matt. 3:16), during Jesus' temptation in the wilderness (Luke 4:1), as a guide for the Church (John 16:13), and as a power that makes non-Hebrew Christians acceptable to God (Rom. 15:16).

Since the Holy Spirit, like God, exists in a plane of reality outside the human, we cannot explain him in rational, scientific terms. One way to approach this formidable challenge is through an analogy that compares the work of the Holy Spirit to a microwave oven. The mysterious capability of this appliance changes what we put in it without visible heat or action. The Holy Spirit operates that way. By other than rationally understandable means, it can change people, sometimes instantly—giving wisdom, love, courage, skill, or faith in ways that surprise both those who receive these gifts and those who observe them.

Since the Holy Spirit is God, we do not need to review the qualities already noted in the first two aspects of God's three-part personality. Rather, we will note only those attributes that are particularly evident in the Holy Spirit.

Power

"But you shall receive power when the Holy Spirit has come upon you" (Acts 1:8).

The English word that describes the most obvious attribute of the Holy Spirit is *power*. Paul said that his speaking ability did not come from wisdom but from the power of the Spirit (I Cor. 2:4). That power appears among the early Christians in numerous ways—in physical healings, in love for those who tried to kill them, in psychological healings, in moral courage, in the ability to preach in unlearned languages, in bold actions, in fervent feelings, and in unintelligible ecstatic utterances during worship services. Although they were ordinary people, these Christians, through an energy beyond their own, began accomplishing things they had previously assumed impossible. They discovered blossoming within their own experience the truth of what one of the Old Testament prophets had said: "Not by might, nor by power, but by my Spirit, says the Lord of hosts" (Zech. 4:6).

Distortions: We distort the biblical meaning of Holy Spirit when we mistake emotional feelings for spiritual wisdom from God, try to use the Spirit for our purposes instead of allowing the Spirit to use us for God's purposes. We also distort the power of the Spirit if we decide that the charismatic experience of speaking in tongues distinguishes Christians from non-Christians, that tongue speaking is the most important gift of the Spirit, or that certain gifts possessed by some of the early Christians, like handling poisonous snakes, should be normative for all Christians today.

Montanus, a church leader in the second century, A.D.,developed a large following that exhibited the same beliefs and behaviors as we see in the Charismatic Movement in our day. The dramatic gifts they experienced included "prophecy" and "tongues," which they believed were signs of the end of time. Montanus claimed direct revelation from God through the gift of the Holy Spirit. He taught that in the "new age of the Spirit" Montanist prophets and prophetesses were speaking God's words of special new revelation. He divided Christians into two groups, "spiritual Christians" and "carnal Christians" who had only the Scriptures. Montanism was declared a heresy. The Council of Constantinople (381 A.D.) recommended that church leaders should place repentant Montanists in an intensive program of scriptural study to correct their misunderstandings of the nature of the Holy Spirit.[1]

The Charismatic Movement has made important contributions to contemporary Christian churches. When it moves over the border into seeing personal revelations as more valid than Scripture and more important than Christian love, it becomes a distorted heresy of the Holy Spirit.

A Power for All Christians

"And Peter said to them, 'Repent and be baptized every one of you in the name of Jesus Christ for the forgiveness of your sins; and you shall receive the gift of the Holy Spirit. For the promise is to you and to your children and to all that are far off, everyone whom the Lord our God calls to him'" (Acts 2:38-39).

Distortions: We distort the biblical meaning of Holy Spirit by thinking that we receive the Holy Spirit at a time other than our initial decision to connect with Christ, that only a few people receive the Holy Spirit, or that we receive the Holy Spirit only by performing certain religious rituals.

Biblical Christianity says that by making a connection with God, all of us can receive the power of the Holy Spirit—a spirit that can empower us to think, become, and do that which would otherwise be impossible to us.

A Renewable Power

"And when they had prayed, the place in which they were gathered together was shaken; and they were filled with the Holy Spirit and spoke the word of God with boldness" (Acts 4:31).

Some, if not most, of the persons in the group described in this verse were surely present at Pentecost, where the phrase "And they were all filled with the Holy Spirit"(Acts 2:4) also appears. The experience of receiving the Holy Spirit is not like a one-act play that is performed for one night only; this is a renewable energy resource that can fill and refill.

Distortions: The idea that we receive the Holy Spirit only once in a lifetime. Paul tells the Christians at Ephesus to be filled with the Spirit (Eph. 5:18)—he says earlier in the same letter that they have already received the Spirit (Eph. 1:13). The New Testament writers do not see the "baptism of the Holy Spirit" as uniquely different from all other experiences with the Holy Spirit. "Baptism of the Holy Spirit" and "Filled with the Holy Spirit" sometimes describe exactly the same event (compare Acts 1:5; 2:4).

A Power That Increases through Prayer

"All those with one accord devoted themselves to prayer. . . . And they were all filled with the Holy Spirit" **(Acts 1:14; 2:4).**

Again and again, the various New Testament writers report the giving of the Holy Spirit to people who had been praying.

Distortions: The idea that we can by much praying control what God's Spirit will do or give us. Like the need to turn on a TV set to receive the signal that has been in the air all the time, the attitude of the heart strengthens the likelihood of receiving the Holy Spirit. But we cannot manipulate or control the giving of that signal.

A Power That Increases through Obedience

"And we are witnesses to these things, and so is the Holy Spirit whom God has given to those who obey him" (Acts 5:32).

Distortions: The idea that we can manipulate and use the Spirit for our own purposes.

The Spirit is given primarily to accomplish God's purposes, not to make us feel better or merely as a cosmic taxi cab to help us arrive at some hoped for destination.

A Power That Communicates Christ

"But you shall receive power when the Holy Spirit has come upon you; and you shall be my witnesses in Jerusalem and in all Judea and Samaria and to the end of the earth" (Acts 1:8).

Distortions: The idea that the Holy Spirit is a spiritual back rub whose only purpose is to help us feel good.

Luke is not the only writer who says the Spirit is given to empower Christians to communicate Christ to others. John and Paul emphasize this, too.

A Power That Connects People with Christ

"No one can come to me unless the Father who sent me draws him" (John 6:44).

Distortions: The idea that we can control by our own efforts and methods who connects with Christ.

When Martin Luther and other great Christian leaders taught that we cannot come to a Christ connection unless the Holy Spirit empowers us, they were standing on firm biblical ground: "no one can say 'Jesus is Lord' except by the Holy Spirit" (I Cor. 12:3).

In the Scripture record, we often see that the Holy Spirit draws people out of their disconnectedness and toward Christ by one of two means: the written word (Philip and the Ethiopian by the side of the road in Acts 8:27) or the spoken word (as in Acts 16:4). But the Holy Spirit can also work through personal life experiences and in other ways to move into the consciousness of persons outside of Christ and create in them new ways of being and acting in their lives. Because God is God, he is not limited in the ways by which he can touch people.

A Power That Gives Love

"God's love has been poured into our hearts through the Holy Spirit which has been given to us" (Rom. 5:5).

Distortions: The idea that God tells us to judge people and tell them the right way to live without also telling us to love them.

Paul says that the Spirit's gifts include faith and hope, but that the Spirit's greatest gift is love (I Cor.12:31; 13:1,13). When John Wesley said that a Methodist is one who has "the love of God shed abroad in his heart by the Holy Ghost given unto him," he was saying the same thing.[2] Through the Holy Spirit, God empowers us to extend his love in word and deed to other persons, even those whose views and actions are quite different from our own.

The Power That Gives Spiritual Abilities

To each is given the manifestation of the Spirit for the common good. To one is given through the Spirit the utterance of wisdom . . . to another faith . . . to another gifts of healing . . . to another prophecy. . . . All these are inspired by one and the same Spirit who apportions to each one individually as he wills (I Cor. 12:7-11).

Distortions: The idea that the gifts of the Spirit are for my personal benefit, rather than for the common good.

Power That Improves Personality

"But the fruit of the Spirit is love, joy, peace, patience, kindness, goodness, faithfulness, gentleness, self-control" (Gal. 5:22-23).

Distortions: The idea that the fruit of the Spirit is knowing the right rules rather than letting God's Spirit shine through us.

People who believe they have received the Holy Spirit benefit from a frequent personality checkup. If several items on Paul's list noted above are missing, the spirit they have may be something other than the Holy Spirit.

The Power That Gives Perfect Advice

"And I will pray the Father, and he will give you another Counselor, to be with you for ever, even the Spirit of truth . . . he will teach you all things, and bring to your remembrance all that I have said to you" (John 14:16-17, 26).

Distortions: The idea that each of us should decide by rational thinking the truth about every personal and church issue we face, without dependence upon God's Spirit.

The Spirit prepared Peter for the coming of Cornelius' servants (Acts 10:19), guided Paul to Troas (Acts 16:6), and warned Paul that he would be imprisoned in Jerusalem (Acts 20:23). When we open our minds to receive him, the mind of Christ comes to our consciousness through the Holy Spirit. This does not eliminate the need for rational thinking. The Spirit strengthens our rational-thinking ability by adding new insights. The Spirit enables us to add God's truth to our mind's truth.

The Invisible Transformer

Christianity is a relationship with God in which we try to discover what Jesus said and did, then attempt to live in a way that says and does those things. We cannot accomplish that without a power beyond our own wisdom and ability. How can we attain the love of Albert Schwietzer, the positive attitude of Norman Vincent Peale, the self-esteem of Robert Schuller, the intellect of Paul Tillich, the evangelistic ability of Billy Graham, and the quiet trust of E. Stanley Jones? Only by having the mind of Christ, and that comes to us only through the power of the Holy Spirit.

Oceanographer Jacques Cousteau tells about a zoo aquarium that ran short of seawater. During that time, they received a shipment of live saltwater invertebrates—lovely anemone and delicate feather-duster worms. The aquarium supervisor decided that they would have to manufacture some seawater by adding salt to ordinary tap water. It did not work. The sea creatures began dying. In desperation, the supervisor decided to dump the tiny amount of real seawater they had left in storage into the aquarium. It worked. The marine life stopped dying. Cousteau said that each drop of seawater obviously contains an invisible spark that we do not understand. When those drops are added to ordinary salted water, they bring life-giving qualities.

Jesus is God's idea of what people can be like. Through the Holy Spirit, God makes the life-giving qualities of Jesus' life available to our life.

Discovery Questions for Group Study

1. Does the Bible report other attributes of the Holy Spirit that are not on this list?

2. Ask everyone in the group to take turns sharing the attributes on this list that are especially meaningful to them. Ask those who

are willing to share experiences or ideas which make that attribute meaningful to them.

3. Is there one or more attribute on this list that you think does not belong here?

4. Are there other contemporary distortions of biblical truth about the Holy Spirit that are not noted?

5. Which of the distortions do you think are most common in our community? Our denomination?

PART II

THE SPOKES

*HOW WE CONNECT
WITH BIBLICAL CHRISTIANITY*

CHAPTER 4

GOD'S MAGNETIC FORCE FIELD

A little boy watched in amazement as a huge electromagnetic crane lifted a ton of scrap metal and placed it in a railroad car. "How does it do that?" the boy asked his father.

"It's magnetic," the father, who was an electrical engineer, replied. "The electricity creates a magnetic force field that makes the scrap iron stick to the electromagnet on the boom of the crane."

"I see that it sticks, but how does it work?" the boy said.

Our world has countless invisible, yet powerful, experiences that we cannot fully grasp by rational means. Radio waves, fax machines, x-rays, TV satellite signals—we know from the evidence that they work; yet, most of us cannot fully explain them. One of the four spokes by which human personality connects with the hub of Christianity (God) is like that—observable but not fully explainable.

Jesus said that God is real and that we can experience his presence in our lives. In communicating this conviction, Jesus used a three-word phrase more than 110 times in the New Testament records: Kingdom of God. But what, exactly, do those three words mean? Because we cannot fully explain them with our present knowledge systems, we must turn to analogies. Some people find it helpful to think of the kingdom of God as a new level of consciousness: They see it as a major shift in thinking, similar to what we all experience in other areas of our lives. For example, on the day that we fall in love, we become entirely different persons. Everything changes. Our thinking and behavior come under the control of a whole new perspective. We look at the world through new mental lenses. We enter a new level of consciousness.

That kind of extraordinary shift in thinking does sound similar to what Jesus was asking that day at the seashore when he said to Peter, "Follow me." It sounds like what Jesus was asking that day at the tax office in Capernaum when he said to Matthew, "Follow me." He was inviting them to do much more than thoughtfully examine a new theory; he was inviting them to enter a new level of consciousness that would change their perspectives, priorities, and behaviors. This "new level of consciousness" explanation also matches two of Jesus' frequently quoted statements about the kingdom: "The kingdom of God is within you" (Luke 17:21, KJV); "Unless one is born anew, he cannot see the kingdom of God" (John 3:3). Along with its helpfulness, however, this "new level of consciousness" analogy has one weakness: It fails to communicate the fact that the kingdom of God is outside of us as well as within us. It is not *just* a level of consciousness; it is also a tangible reality that exists outside of our consciousness.

Other people find it more helpful to describe the kingdom of God as a magnetic force field that we enter by choice. This analogy locates the kingdom outside of human personality as well as within. It sees the kingdom as more than a psychological mood, state, or attitude; it is a powerful force field, whether we decide to connect with it or not.

Yet, these and all other analogies fail to totally define and describe the kingdom of God. The kingdom, like God, is a field of reality that interfaces with our human field of experience like a large circle intersects with a smaller circle at only one small section. The kingdom of God is connected with but also beyond our plane of reality: "My kingship is not of this world" (John 18:36), Jesus said. "The wind blows where it wills, and you hear the sound of it, but you do not know whence it comes or whither it goes; so it is with every one who is born of the Spirit" (John 3:8).

However we decide to define or describe it, an invisible spiritual reality exists alongside of and intertwined with visible physical reality. Recognizing this and deciding to move close enough so that the metal of our personality can enter and experience this spiritual force field is one of the four spokes by which we grasp and hold on to biblical Christianity (Mark 12:34). Jesus urges us to seek the kingdom (Luke 12:22-31). He says it is available to everyone and that we enter it, not by knowledge, ritual, or aid of a priest, but with childlike trust (Mark 10:13-16). Early preaching was about the Kingdom (Acts 8:12, 19:8, 28:31). Paul says that the things of the Spirit of God are spiritually discerned (I Cor. 2:14). *Biblical Christianity is, therefore, centered on the spiritual reality of the kingdom of God.* Unless we enter the electromagnetic force field of the kingdom, the kingdom cannot enter us.

The Great Paradox

More and more people believe in spiritual reality these days. According to a Gallup Survey, 49 percent of British people have had experiences of spirits or forces beyond themselves. Ninety-four percent of Americans say they believe in God, and 90 percent say they pray to God.[1] More than one in three Americans say that God speaks directly to them. Belief in angels among American teenagers increased from 64 percent in 1978 to 74 percent in 1988.[2] Many people say they have experienced some form of ESP, the communication of thoughts from one mind to another over great distances by other than observable means. In every large city, thousands of people meet each week to confess the breaking of their addiction to alcohol by divine power. More and more people agree with what the Queen said to Alice in *Through the Looking Glass*: "Why, sometimes, I've believed as many as six impossible things before breakfast."

Concurrent with this public increase of belief in spiritual reality, however, many church leaders have, during the past few decades, diminished their emphasis on spiritual reality. After World War II, many people became increasingly fascinated with the possibility that science, rational thinking, and progressive human ingenuity could solve every problem. Caught up in this way of viewing reality, many church leaders seemed to increasingly communicate the idea that the spiritual is an outdated, unneeded, and overly emotional inclination of uneducated personalities. In response to this trend among church leaders, many young adults shifted away from their denomination of birth toward newer denominations that give greater emphasis to spiritual reality. In this respect, the much publicized decline of mainline church membership stems from a loss of religion itself. Without confidence in the supernatural (God and spiritual reality), Christianity has little to offer people that they cannot get elsewhere in a superior form. They can get instruction in rational thinking from educational institutions, and they can get emotional needs met at football games.

Inflationary Ideas

In the declining years of the great Roman Empire, a problem called inflation began destroying the middle-class yeoman farmers who had built that mighty republic. The Roman coin was a denarius, a little silver coin about the size of a dime. The emperors discovered a simple way to generate extra funds. Every time the coin came back through the treasury, they snipped off the edge and put it back into circulation slightly smaller. They melted the clippings down to make extra denarii. It was a simpler system than the Federal Reserve, but it had a similar effect. More and more denarii were chasing the same amount of goods. Many religious leaders have in recent decades followed a similar pattern. Snipping the edges off biblical Christianity, they have provided smaller and smaller ideas to people increasingly hungry for knowledge about spiritual reality. Historically, this distortion of the spiritual reality taught by Jesus and biblical Christianity has been called Pelagianism, a name taken from a heresy of early centuries. To the Pelagian, supernatural activity is a myth. The miracles reported in Scripture must be explained as superstitious inventions or inaccurate reports. Christ was just a great man, and the resurrection was a fantasy of hopeful followers.

A pastor tells about attending a banquet where all the sugar holders contained little sugar envelopes, but they were empty of sugar. A religious institution devoid of conviction about spiritual reality is like an empty sugar envelope. Like false advertising, it promises what it does not deliver. In a highly secularized society hungry for re-spiritualization, churches that major in the spiritual reality dimension of biblical Christianity are likely to flourish. Those that do not tend to disappear.

Both inside and outside of organized religion, another common distortion of spiritual reality is materialism—people who reach out for meaning by trying to fill the emptiness of their lives with purchases. Near the end of the Oregon Trail is a tragic monument. The tombstone is erected to a man who died of thirst only a few hundred yards from a major stream. So it is with many church members who stand so near to the power of spiritual reality but do not see it. Overwhelmed with the dry flats of anxiety, boredom, or hopelessness, they try to quench their thirst with the mirage of materialism. They think that possessions can bring meaning and abundant life. In so doing, they miss the water of life that is only a few steps away.

More Than Meets the Eye

Jesus says that life at its unseen roots is spiritual—that a spiritual reality below the surface feeds the rest of life. Historian Arnold Toynbee was pointing in that direction when he said that only six men in history have found the secret of life: Jesus, Moses, Buddha, Lincoln, St. Francis, and Gandhi. They gave top priority to the unseen world of spiritual reality. They understood fully that "we look not to the things that are seen but to the things that are unseen; for the things that are seen are transient, but the things that are unseen are eternal" (II Cor. 4:18).

Tolstoy tells about a Russian youth who was put on trial because he was a conscientious objector to war. When he stated his position in the courtroom, the boy said that he based it on the demands of Christ. The judge responded, "Yes, I understand, but you must be realistic. These laws you are talking about are the laws of the Kingdom of God and it has not come yet!"

"Sir," said the young man, "I recognize that it has not come for you, nor yet for Russia, nor for the world. But it has come for me."[3] Jesus said that it can come for each of us. When we choose to enter God's magnetic force field, we come into contact with a more powerful shaper of reality than anything we can see with our eyes.

The spiritual reality of God's kingdom is already here (Luke 11:20). He wants to give it to us (Luke 12:32). When we decide to enter it, it will enter us (Luke 17:20-21).

Discovery Questions for Group Study

1. In addition to the two mentioned in this chapter, are there other contemporary distortions (heresies) of biblical truth regarding spiritual reality?

2. Ask everyone in the group who is comfortable in doing so to tell about a time in their life when they experienced spiritual reality.

3. Ask everyone in the group to take turns sharing the primary way in which they are best able to come into contact with spiritual reality.

4. Do you think that the young adults in our society are more serious about spiritual reality than their parents and grandparents were? Illustrate.

5. Do you think leaders in our denomination put too little or too much emphasis on spiritual reality? Illustrate.

CHAPTER 5

WINDOW, MIRROR, AND PICTURE

A seven-year-old gave his grandmother a gift Bible. She barely kept her composure as she opened the cover and read the hand-printed words in the front. He had carefully copied them from the fly leaf of a valuable book in his father's library: "With the compliments and best wishes of the author."

That naive inscription, while not exactly appropriate, is accurate. It is the invisible autograph in the front of all Bibles. It also tells us why this book is another major spoke by which people connect with God. Through Jesus, we know what God is like. The Bible is the only written record of what Jesus said and did. It is therefore our most objective source for knowing the mind of God, how we can relate to God, and how our lives can have purpose, meaning, and power. While sincere Christians do not always agree on how to interpret everything in the Bible (any more than Supreme Court Justices always agree on how to interpret the Constitution), Scripture remains the ultimate authority for Christian thinking and action. *Biblical Christianity is by nature Bible-centered.*

We get this pattern from Jesus himself. He used Scripture as an authority to debate the Pharisees and Sadducees, pointing out errors in the way they had interpreted the nature of God. He warns the disciples against relaxing the standard of scriptural authority (Matt. 5:17-20). He places his own words on the same authoritative level as the Old Testament: "Heaven and Earth will pass away, but my words will not pass away" (Mark 13:31).

John Calvin, one of the Protestant reformers, was following this pattern when he stood firmly on the Bible as a foundation for authoritative teaching. He believed that Scripture is the instrument by which God dispenses the illumination of his Spirit to believers.[1]

Martin Luther took the same position: "You are so to deal with the Scriptures that you bear in mind that God Himself is saying this."[2] John Wesley built Methodism on the same authority foundation: "We believe the written word of God to be the only and sufficient rule both of Christian faith and practice."[3]

Window to God

Every book helps us get acquainted with the author's thinking. That is true in an even more powerful way when we read the Bible. The author is always present when we read it. Through these pages, we can see beyond the present moment in time. We see beyond our present level of consciousness into the unlimited possibilities of spiritual reality. Substituting something else for the authority of the Bible is therefore among the greatest of sins. It pulls a curtain over one of the windows through which we can catch a glimpse of God.

A self-confessed agnostic who has spent years teaching illiterate people to read says that he is always amazed at the answer most of them give when asked why they want to learn to read. Rather than saying they want to make more money, most of them say, "I want to read the Bible."[4] Why do these people who have so many other needs—like how to read a medicine bottle, or an application for financial assistance—respond this way? Because they know the Bible is our primary source of authority, not just for biblical Christianity, but for life. They know that this book is a window to God, and they want to raise the blinds.

Mirror to Self

The Bible is more than a window: It is also a mirror in which we see ourselves more clearly than in any other book. A tradition among Jewish scholars says that in the Torah (first five books of the Old Testament) every word and every letter has 100,000 layers of meaning. Therefore, if you want to find out what one word of the Torah means, you need a committee of at least 100,000 in order to bring it all together. That is close to what the New Testament writers mean when they call Scripture the "living Word." It speaks personally to each of us. We don't just interpret the Bible; it interprets us to ourselves. A weather forecaster said to a friend, "I want to invite you to go to church with me Sunday. There is a 30 percent chance of inspiration." When we open the Bible, we look into the world's finest mirror. Our chances of inspiration increase to 100 percent.

Picture of Christ

The more than 700,000 words in the Bible accomplish many different things for a reader. None is more valuable than the picture of Christ we see in these pages. After Jesus' resurrection, the disciples found themselves walking with a stranger on the road to Emmaus. After he shared Scripture with them, they knew it was Jesus. In our day, that situation is reversed. Instead of Christ opening the Scripture to us; the Scripture opens Christ to us.

As a couple left the Pennsylvania Turnpike about 2:00 A.M. and headed through the mountains, they ran into dense fog. The familiar road evaporated into detours around construction sites. Creeping cautiously up a side road, they felt it turn into ruts. Since by now they could barely see the hood of the car, they stopped. The man thought he saw a sign ahead. Getting out of the car, he groped toward the sign, finally reached it, and struck a match. In spite of their predicament, he burst out laughing. The sign read, "Smokey the Bear says put out that match!" With different people saying different things about Christ, we can get lost in the fog. But the road has some reliable signs. One of these is the Bible. All we have to do is stop and light a match.

Distortions of Biblical Authority

The ways in which people distort this window, mirror, and picture are almost endless. The following list contains some of the most common of these.

Disregarding the Bible. The prophet Jeremiah spoke against prophets who replaced Scripture with dreams (Jer. 23:25-32).

Astrology and downright disregard of scripture do that in our day. More than two-thirds of U.S. adults (68 percent) read at least some part of some newspaper every day. Yet, only 23 percent of church members read the Bible as frequently as once a month.[5] It is the most widely unread best seller. Many people have adopted what amounts to a unilateral, biblical disarmament.

Making the Bible an icon. In some parts of the world, Christians revere icons, or statues, as sacred objects. For some Americans, the Bible fills a similar role. A mother tells of leaving church to travel with her family to attend a baby shower for her sister in a nearby community at 2:00 P.M. Sunday afternoon. As they walked into the shower, she noticed that her eight-year-old was carrying her Bible. "Why on earth are you bringing your Bible in here?" the mother asked. "You should have left it in the car."

The little girl replied, "I like to carry my Bible. It makes me look more sincere."

Taking the Bible literally but not seriously. What happens, for example, if we take all of Jesus' sayings literally? We would see devout people cutting off their hands and pulling their eyes out. After all, is not that what Jesus recommended for lustful thinking and bad behavior (Matt. 5:27-30)? The Bible contains at least eighteen different kinds of literature. The one above is called "hyperbole," an exaggerated statement to make a point. Other literary forms in the Bible include folksongs, parables, allegories, history, biography, laws, poetry, proverbs, speeches, prayers, letters, essays, fables, legends, myths, elegies, and drama. All of these literary forms convey truth. But if we do not understand what kind of literary container this truth is carried in, we can disregard the truth by taking it literally rather than seriously.

Victor Borge once told about the time he and his wife checked into a hotel. The sign in the bathroom said, "Please place the curtains inside the tub." Wanting to be good guests, they obliged, although they could not see why the staff didn't handle this. It took twenty minutes to get that curtain off those little hooks. Then, they didn't know whether the sign meant all the curtains in the suite, or just the shower curtain. To be safe, they put all of them in the tub.

Taking every word of the Bible literally surely cannot be what God expects. God is a more rational thinker than that.

Reading the Bible selectively rather than totally. That lets us take the text "An eye for an eye and a tooth for a tooth" and use it as a justification for vengeance. That lets us take the saying about Ham—that he should be a slave to his brothers—and use it as justification for slavery, as many did before the Civil War. That lets us take the Exodus text "You shall not suffer a witch to live" and use it as a reason for burning people, as it was used in Salem, Massachusetts. That lets us take a verse from Luke 14 that says, when a king has his banquet and invites people in, go out and compel them to come in, and justify procedures like those used in the Spanish Inquisition, which executed people if they did not comply with the invitation.

Allowing academic interpretation to take precedence over biblical truth. The distortions inherent in "form criticism" and other technical systems of biblical interpretation popular among some scholars of recent decades are difficult to see because they are advocated by well-educated people. Under the rubric of academic excellence, these approaches have said in various ways that the Bible is out of date in its language and teachings, and thus impossible to use without appropriate scholarly interpretation. This is a bit like the diner at a luxurious restaurant who insists on discarding the entire trout amandine because he discovers bones in it. Ironically, these scholarly distortions are virtually identical to those of the New Age Movement. Their thinkers find the Scriptures contradictory, impractical, out of date, and based more on subjective experience than objective truth.[6]

Allowing church traditions to take precedence over the Bible. The Bible is not the only truth about God. The truth passed down through the centuries in the container of church traditions also has value. But these traditions so easily become god instead of God. Jesus said, "You have let go of the commands of God and are holding on to the traditions of men" (Mark 7:8). The more we love our church, the more we are tempted in this direction. This is what a layperson was saying to an evaluation committee regarding a student pastor: "He has not impressed us as strongly biblically oriented. He seems to place more reliance on our denomination's position than on scriptural teachings." Martin Luther said the same thing about church leaders during the Protestant Reformation in the sixteenth century.

Allowing personal interpretation to take precedence over the Bible itself. The Bible's truth comes to us through the doorway of our mind. There is therefore no such thing as an uninterpreted Bible verse. We cannot, however, take this fact to mean that all the Bible's truth is dependent upon what we think about it. A text cannot mean whatever we decide it means. A young couple taking their infant to the church nursery chuckled at the Bible verse over the door: "We shall all sleep, but we shall all be changed" (I Cor. 15:51). Not all of the personal interpretations people take from Scripture are that harmless. Some New Age Movement leaders see an interpretation they thought of last week as having more authority than the convictions of centuries of biblical scholarship. Some thinkers from the existentialist school of theology have taken the position that biblical truth cannot be truth unless I decide it is truth. That is like having a map that says "you are here" at seventeen different locations. If we can be anywhere and be right, then why cannot we be everywhere and be right? Biblical Christianity is not that flexible in its view of truth.

In the second century, Marcion decided to remove all the Judaizing passages from the Gospel of Luke and Paul's letters. He was sure that the God of the Old Testament was too strong on justice and wanted to be sure that Christians emphasized love and grace. When church leaders declared Marcion a heretic in 143 A.D., they were saying that some parts of the Christian authority system are not a matter of subjective opinion. Two plus two equals four is a very narrow view of truth, but some truth is exactly that narrow. Unless our opinions are coupled with a solid knowledge of the Bible, the results are similar to a phrase common in the computer industry—"trash in, trash out."

The final exam for biblical interpretation. Jesus said that loving God and loving people are the main things. The Bible expands on the why and the how of that. If our interpretations do not point in the direction of the Christ whose principle directive was "love one another; even as I have loved you" (John 13:34), we have strayed off the path and run the risk of driving over the cliffs into a Grand Canyon of error.

God's Mountain

A woman who had lived in Colorado Springs for only a few weeks had trouble finding her way around. Soon, however, she learned to orient herself by locating Pike's Peak, which looms 14,110 feet above the city. One day her husband was surprised to answer the phone and hear his wife say, "Come and get me. I can't find my way home."

"How come?" the husband asked. "You always have before."

"But it's cloudy today," she said. "I can't see the mountain."

The Bible is the mountain by which we can most clearly see God, ourselves, and Jesus Christ. If we lose sight of the mountain, we have trouble finding our way home.

Discovery Questions for Group Thinking

1. Do you think the Bible has other important functions besides serving as a window to God, a mirror to self, and a picture of Christ? If you do share these with the group.

2. Ask everyone in the group to take turns sharing the way(s) in which the Bible has been the most meaningful to them personally.

3. Can you think of other contemporary distortions of biblical authority that were not cited in this chapter?

4. Which of the distortions do you think are most common in our community? Our denomination?

CHAPTER 6

AIMING OUR SATELLITE DISH

A hospital chaplain who carried an electronic pager was visiting two patients. When asked to pray with them, he was interrupted when the pager on his belt emitted a "beep, beep, beep." One of the patients said, "Never knew a pastor with such direct contact!" Actually, however, all of us have that kind of access. God is always available for consultation. Through experiencing spiritual reality, we know God is here. Through the window of the Bible, we see what God is like. *Through prayer, we can talk with God.*

Although prayer, like God, cannot be fully explained by rational means, brain-wave research is beginning to uncover physiological evidence for how our part of this conversation works. The Alpha wave of seven to fourteen cycles per second produces more "brain energy" than the Beta level of fourteen to twenty-one cycles per second. Beta waves happen when we are in a normal conscious state like physical activity and problem solving. Alpha waves happen when we are tranquil and relaxed, with eyes closed, as in a state of prayer or meditation. God is apparently trying to communicate with us all the time. When we set our receiver on Alpha, the communication can connect. God is always sending his signal. Prayer is the satellite dish by which we receive it.

The Pattern

"And in the morning, a great while before day, he rose and went out to a lonely place, and there he prayed" (Mark 1:35).

This pattern appears repeatedly in the biblical record. Jesus prayed before he made important decisions. When his disciples were fearful, Jesus prayed for them. Because of his close friends' grief, Jesus prayed. He even prayed for those who drove nails through his hands. *Biblical Christianity is, therefore, prayer-centered.*

The Purpose

The disciples soon saw that prayer was the crux of Jesus' strength and asked him to teach them how to receive this power (Luke 11:1-4 and Matt. 6:9-15). Nowhere else do we find the disciples requesting instructions in how to do something. They do not say, "Teach us how to preach." They do not say, "Tell us how to grow a church." They do not say, "Show us how to perform miracles." Their request for instruction in prayer shows that the disciples recognized what Christians through the centuries have repeatedly rediscovered. Prayer is the most basic action of Christianity and the most basic form of worship. Jesus said that loving God is the most important commandment. How do you love God? Primarily through worship. How do you worship? Primarily through prayer.

Prayer has innumerable values. Through prayer we can receive guidance, strength, and courage. Through prayer we can overcome doubt, reduce stress, discover new insights, improve our personality, increase the quality of our interpersonal relations, and improve our health. In the "Additional Comments" blank in a congregational opinion poll, a woman wrote a phrase containing a spelling error: "We need more prayer and medication." That spelling error may have produced a more profound observation than the one she had intended to write. Prayer is like medication. It can transform our consciousness by opening wider the door that lets God's power into our thinking and behavior. Through prayer, we can raise our insight to God's level of consciousness.

The Power

"Ask, and it will be given you; seek, and you will find; knock, and it will be opened to you" (Matt. 7:7).

God keeps this promise in two ways, by changing our circumstances and by changing the way we feel about our circumstances.

Sometimes, God changes our circumstances. A study published in the *Journal of the American Medical Association* indicates that hospitalized heart patients have fewer medical complications when prayed for. In this study, a San Francisco coronary care unit physician randomly assigned one-half of 393 patients to be prayed for during a ten-month experiment. Patients were not told which group they were in. The people praying knew the patients' first names and got updates on their condition but had no contact with them. The two groups of patients were equally sick when they entered the hospital, but those who were prayed for had "significantly lower severity scores" during their hospital stay.[1] Why do these kinds of results not happen every time we pray? We are not sure. We are, however, sure that prayer, in some way not explainable by present knowledge, gets results that have no other plausible explanation.

The study of quantum mechanics may eventually tell us something of what Jesus understood about prayer. Scientists say that the implications of quantum mechanics are psychedelic. It is beginning to appear that not only do we influence our reality; to some degree, we create it. John Wheeler, a well-known physicist at Princeton, raises the question of whether the universe may in some strange sense be brought into being by our participation.[2] This is exactly what Jesus taught concerning the power of prayer. We may be able to manipulate reality more than we ever imagined.

Sometimes, God changes the way we feel about our circumstances. A physician describing the tendency of persons to come back again and again to a certain type of drug, said, "They are attracted to it because of its mood-altering capability. They become addicted to the mood alteration that they experience." Pharmaceuticals are not the only elements capable of mood alteration. Alcohol can alter mood. Exercise can alter mood. Prayer can alter mood. In addition to encouraging people to stay away from mood-altering drugs, perhaps we should urge them to develop a positive addiction to the mood-altering states that come through exercise and prayer. People who regularly practice prayer are much less likely to need drugs. Their mood is already altered, and in a much healthier manner.

The Prescription

Harry Emerson Fosdick, pastor of the great Riverside Church, New York City, was standing by the rail admiring Niagara Falls. The man next to him said, "You know, right there is the greatest unused power in all the world."

Fosdick replied, "No, I'm afraid I'll have to disagree with you. The greatest unused power in all the world is prayer!"[3]

Embedded in Jesus' parable about the friend who came knocking at the door at midnight to ask for three loaves of bread is a one-word prescription that unlocks the power of prayer. The word is persistence (Luke 11:8). The rest of the New Testament expands on and illustrates that word in various ways. The Thessalonian writer, for example, puts it this way: "Pray without ceasing" (I Thess. 5:17). However we put it, the key to prayer is doing it. If prayer is the power, persistence is the prescription for its use. God already knows what we need, but he does not begin reorganizing our circumstances and the way we feel about our circumstances unless we persistently ask. When John Wesley said that God does nothing except by prayer, he did not mean that God is helpless without us. He meant that prayer, like conversation, requires two people. When one stops talking, the other stops listening.

Distortions

We can distort Jesus' simple prescription about persistent prayer in several ways:

1. By treating God like a cosmic taxicab that we hail when we need a lift.

2. By doing all the talking in prayer, and failing to listen.

3. By substituting—asking God to help people instead of responding to God's call that we help them.

4. By repeatedly asking God's forgiveness for something instead of changing our actions.

5. By asking God to be our "health-and-wealth Santa Claus."

6. By feeling that we can only pray in church or other special places.

7. By the desire to bend God to our will rather than allowing him to mold us to his will.

8. By praying to other gods, like astrology, luck, money, or status.

9. By thinking that God must always answer every prayer with a yes.

10. By feeling that God must give us instant results.

11. By asking for help only with our own problems, without asking God's help for other people.

12. By making prayer a selfish habit rather than a self-giving, yielding habit.

13. By praying without forgiving the people who hurt us.

14. By asking for help in big things but not smaller, daily matters.

Spending too much space in discussing these distortions could, in itself, become a distortion. Each of these arises from a more basic distortion. Failure to be persistent in prayer is an invisible form of atheism. Prayer is a language of dependence. When we pray, we are saying, "I believe I am not alone in the universe. I believe God is real. I believe I cannot make it to wholeness by myself." When we do not pray persistently, we are saying, "I can do it by myself." This invisible atheism of unexpressed prayer blocks us from biblical Christianity, because it blocks us from a relationship with God. If we never talked with our spouse, we could hardly expect a positive relationship. The same goes for us and God.

Unlimited Provisions

A few years ago, a rescue party found an eight-year-old boy sitting on a rock beside a burned plane twelve miles north of Flin Flan, Manitoba. He and his father had been fishing. On the way home, the plane crashed, killing his father instantly. The boy, hungry and afraid, waited fifteen days for his mother to come for him—while the Royal Canadian Air Force and civilian planes scoured 70,000 square miles looking for the downed plane. Finally, a commercial airline pilot saw him standing on the rock, waving for help. This experience was even more tragic because the boy need not have become emaciated for lack of food. Near the plane, the rescue party found a survival kit that had been thrown free on impact. It contained a twenty-four-day supply of rations, but the boy had not known what was in it.[4]   Follow the pattern and the prescription with persistence, and you receive the power and the provisions. Go it alone, and you will survive, but not nearly as well.

Discovery Questions for Group Study

1. Does the Bible report other values of prayer not noted in this chapter?

2. Ask those in the group who are comfortable in doing so to share their most meaningful experience with prayer.

3. Can you think of other distortions of prayer not listed in this chapter?

4. Ask those in the group who feel comfortable in doing so to share the one thing that has most helped them to be persistent in prayer.

5. Ask those who are willing to do so to share the times of day and the ways they have found most beneficial in developing the habit of daily prayer.

CHAPTER 7

LET'S BE REASONABLE

In 1870, one out of every 762 Americans was enrolled in college. In 1987, one out of every twenty Americans was a college or university student. Approximately 63 percent of all high school graduates now attend college, and 30 percent of them earn at least a bachelor's degree. And yet, concurrent with this rapid rise in educational levels, we see an epidemic of unintelligent behavior—drug use, alcoholism, violence, child abuse, and high divorce rates.

This strange paradox in which we can see both the value and the limitations of rational thinking is also obvious in Christianity. Christian faith always involves rational thinking. Reason is the tool by which our mind experiences spiritual reality, understands the Bible, and relates to God through prayer. *Biblical Christianity is reason-centered.* And yet, reason has enormous limitations. Educated Christians violated Christ's law of love by permitting the Spanish Inquisition. Using reason, they practiced slavery. Using reason, they call each other names because of disagreements regarding biblical interpretation.

The Role of Reason

Rational thinking is a tool of biblical Christianity in three primary ways:

Understanding. Reason is our means of understanding the benefits of a faith relationship with God. In Jesus, God revealed himself (John 1:18). In Jesus' teachings, God told us how we can pattern our life after his. A car's gas tank is the way it receives gasoline, just as the mind is the way we receive these truths about God.

Deciding. Reason is our means of deciding to establish a faith relationship with God. Knowing is never enough. After we understand, we have to decide to act on what we know. Even Jesus had to decide. After his baptism, "The Spirit immediately drove him into the wilderness" (Mark 1:12). There, he struggled with the temptation to put something else ahead of God. He had seen spiritual reality, calling it the kingdom of God. He already knew the Old Testament Scriptures. He had related to God through prayer. But he still had to choose. He could not drift into a firm God connection. He had to decide, and reason was his tool for deciding.

Directing. Reason is our means of directing the growth of our faith relationship with God. After the initial decision to connect with God, we must keep on choosing the ways in which we will allow that faith relationship to influence our life. That, too, happens through reason. In Wesley's famous quadrilateral for the Christian life, church tradition is one-fourth of the equation (along with personal experience, the Bible, and reason). But the light of tradition, like the light of the Bible, comes to us through the lens of reason. Do I or do I not want to conform to this Christian tradition? When we answer that question, we are using the authority of reason.

Distortions of Reason

Both within and outside of biblical Christianity, people distort the tool of reason in many ways. Reason can, for example, become a means of criticizing faith and judging it irrational. The atheist uses reason that way. So does the Christian who denies the possibility of the resurrection and Jesus' miracles. By believing in syncretism, reason can say that our spiritual choices are unlimited, that all world religions are equal. By believing in pluralism, reason can say we need to make room in the tent of faith for every kind of belief. If we dissect and analyze each of these contemporary distortions, they all come down to one thing: *Reason as a substitute for faith.*

During the seventeenth century, a cluster of assumptions about reality called "The Enlightenment" began to displace basic Christian beliefs for many people. The Enlightenment stressed confidence in human reason, science, and the possibilities of technology. During this period, the philosophy of Deism began to replace biblical Christianity for many clergy and laity. In Deism, reason, not the Bible, was the supreme authority. Science, in the hand of rational individuals, became their hope for the future. This substitution of reason for faith continues today. When facing a major life issue, many people are more likely to say, "What does science think and what do I think?" than to say, "What does the Bible say God thinks?"

How, then, does reason fit into biblical Christianity? As a servant. Reason is a servant of our faith relationship with God. When reason becomes more than a servant of faith, it makes faith less than faith. If reason becomes our primary authority for measuring truth, Christian faith deteriorates to a list of principles—rather than a personal relationship with a God whose thoughts are higher than our thoughts (Isa. 55:9).

Reason is a valuable tool in protecting us from developing crazy beliefs, but we must not equate belief with faith. Belief is a rational mental process. Faith is a spiritual process, a relationship with God that is initiated and maintained by our will. The bottom-line goal of biblical Christianity is not rational belief but a faith relationship. Rational belief can help us move toward a faith relationship destination, but it is not the destination—anymore than the North Star is the destination for a ship that uses it as a means of setting the proper course.

Reason and faith have always been nervous partners. A book used in Catholic schools in the United States in the 1880s says, "An open Bible and free interpretation proclaimed by the Reformers, destroys the authority of the Church, and practically makes reason the rule of faith."[1] These Catholic leaders were saying that reason cannot be the final authority for faith—just as the Protestant leaders were saying that Church tradition (a disguised form of reason) cannot be the final authority for faith. Both groups were right.

Four Spokes

The central hub of biblical Christianity is God, Jesus Christ, and the Holy Spirit. Four spokes connect with that hub to produce and enlarge Christian faith:

1. Our recognition of and experience with spiritual reality.

2. The Bible, which transmits the truth about God to us through the Holy Spirit's inspiration of the writers.

3. Prayer, which allows God to communicate with us.

4. Our mind, whose capacity for reasoning allows us to receive and assimilate information.

Remove any one of these four spokes (or depend on one of them alone) and the wheel falls apart. Depending on the experience of spiritual reality alone can deteriorate into the extremes of mysticism and spiritualism. Depending on the Bible alone can deteriorate into worshiping the Bible—or *bibliolatry*—instead of worshiping God. Depending on prayer alone can deteriorate into the extremes of Charismatic emotionalism that border on craziness. Depending on the mind alone can deteriorate into worship of reason—or *rationalatry*—makes us god instead of God.

Beyond Reason

The Christian faith is reasonable, but it is far more than reason. It is a spiritual commitment of the will in which reason plays the role of servant rather than master. A Korean-American clergyman says that one of the major differences between the fast-growing United Methodist Korean congregations in the United States and the typical congregation is the dependence on a biblical faith that transcends rationality and calculation. Korean believers constantly feel something beyond what they rationalize and calculate.

Alvin Jackson, pastor of one of America's fastest-growing Black congregations in Memphis, Tennessee, puts it this way: "If my religion is only in my head, and I lose my head, I will lose my religion."[2]

Discovery Questions for Group Study

1. Do you agree or disagree with the statement that reason is the lens through which all truth comes to us?

2. Ask everyone in the group who is willing to do so to share their opinion regarding how much of a role reason played in their own personal decision to connect with God.

3. If some in the group feel that factors other than reason played a far stronger role in their decision to connect with God, ask them to share their story and their opinions about how that process worked.

4. Of the several items described in the first paragraph of the section entitled "Distortions of Reason," which do you think is the most prevalent distortion in our culture? In our community? In our denomination? In our church?

5. In the section entitled "Four Spokes," which of these do you think receives the greatest emphasis as a means of connecting with God by people in our denomination? In our congregation?

6. Ask everyone in the group to share which of the four spokes he or she relies on the most to connect with God, and why?

PART III

THE WHEEL

HOW BIBLICAL CHRISTIANITY
STRENGTHENS OUR PERSONALITY

CHAPTER 8

ENLARGING OUR CURRENCY

G oing through the customs gate to get on a plane leaving Australia, a tourist was told he needed a departure tax stamp. After listening to the instructions, he went downstairs in the Sydney airport and found the departure tax windows. The fee was $20, and he shoved it across the counter. "No," the agent said, "we don't take U.S., only Australian." The tourist began to panic. The currency exchange bank was in another part of the airport, and the time of his plane's departure was rapidly approaching. He ran to the bank, stood in line, got his money exchanged, ran back to the departure tax window, ran back to the customs gate, and made it to his plane minutes before it took off.

A similar currency transaction happens in the personality of everyone who connects with God. Jesus said in his first sermon, "Repent, for the kingdom of God is at hand" (Mark 1:14). That message still fits. When we see that we cannot get on the plane to a life of meaning and fulfillment with the currency of life priorities we are presently carrying, repentance becomes the only rational alternative. When we recognize that God's kingdom of spiritual reality is here among us and we have not entered it, what else can we say except, "I'm sorry"? *Biblical Christianity is, therefore, repentance-centered.*

The manner in which repentance occurs, however, is often misunderstood by persons who have not experienced it. We do not repent in order to earn a tax stamp that connects us with God. Rather, our repentance is the natural result of making a connection with God. First, we say, "I believe. I believe that God is here and wants to relate to me." As soon as that happens, we feel the truth of what Paul wrote: "All have sinned, and come short of the glory of God" (Rom. 3:23). Seeing that we have willfully lived as if God does not exist, we are ready to say, "God be merciful to me a sinner" (Luke 18:13).

Many people who have not experienced repentance misunderstand the meaning of the word because they misunderstand the meaning of the word *sin*. Sin is not immorality. Sin is self-centeredness. Sin is unbelief. Sin is locking God out of thought and life. Sin is the unwillingness to make God our guiding focus for living. When we make something else the guiding focus of life rather than God, we face eternal death (separation from God). This puts us in hell (where people who live with self at the center and God at the rim go).

Grace

Grace is God's unlimited acceptance, forgiveness, and power that he gives us for new life directions. We do not repent and then experience the feeling of God's grace. Rather, we sense God's grace as we recognize and enter the kingdom of spiritual reality Jesus told us is here. That draws us toward repentance of our self-centeredness—an experience that gives us an even greater capacity for experiencing God's grace of acceptance, forgiveness, and power for new life.

Grace is like a diamond with many facets. It can be described from several different angles: Grace appears first in Jesus Christ, through whom God acted to help people reinstate a relationship with God. That grace is eternally extended, whether we accept it or not. That is what Christmas is all about—the celebration of that gift.

Grace is also like a magnet: It both draws us toward a relationship with God in the kingdom of spiritual reality and gives us a new level of consciousness after we decide to enter that relationship. Augustine, and later Wesley, called this "prevenient grace," a grace that influences our will to move in God's direction. Grace also gives us the power to stay in this new level of consciousness after we decide to enter a relationship with God. Augustine saw that aspect of grace as the gift of perseverance.

A major psychological result of grace is increased feelings of self-esteem and self-worth. All of us need acceptance, either because we received it from our parents and want more of it, or because we were "unblest" by our parents and yearn for it. Grace gives us that when we enter a relationship with God.

Grace is a liquid that pours itself into the shape of our personal need. Therefore, it brings feelings that are described in many different ways by different people—inner peace, a sense of forgiveness, joy, healing from past brokenness, freedom from anxiety, increased love for others, clearer understanding of scriptural truth, a new sense of meaning and purpose, clearer conviction regarding a life calling or vocation, a sense of Christ's presence, a feeling of harmony with the universe, a sense of belonging, an assurance that God will care for every aspect of our future.

Grace always empowers a Christian with special gifts that God calls them to use in his service. For some, that is increased teaching ability, but it can take countless other forms. Some sense and use those gifts more than others, but everyone receives them. For most, those gifts of grace are unobtrusive and little noticed. For others, like John Wesley, they are enormously visible and public: In a letter dated in 1763, Wesley wrote, "The power I have, I never sought. It was the undesired, unexpected result of the work God was pleased to work by me. I have a thousand times sought to devolve it on others; but as yet I cannot."[1]

We receive the feeling of grace in a variety of ways—through prayer, the Bible, worship, sacrament, temperance, Christian fellowship, a personal experience, or casual words of someone through whom God speaks a great truth to us. However the feeling of grace begins, it is always a free gift that we cannot in any way earn or gain by personal effort. As Paul says, your spiritual strength comes as a gift of God (Hebrews 3:9).

Yet, even though grace is free and we cannot earn it, we must open our hearts in order to receive it. A Missouri congregation received from its national denominational office a certificate honoring its significant evangelistic growth for the previous year. Whoever opened the mail apparently thought it was a book they had not ordered, so the package was returned, unopened. When it got back to the national office, it was battered into unusable condition. The frame holding the certificate was cracked and the glass covering it was shattered.

Grace is a description of that transaction by which God gives us, unsolicited, a gift that can change our self-esteem, meet deep psychological needs, and empower us to keep moving in new and positive directions. We can do nothing to stop God from mailing us this gift. He already has. It is his nature to do so. But we can refuse to open our mail. We can return the gift as a sack of broken glass and splintered frame. Repentance is what happens when we decide to open the package and keep the grace.

Conversion

Conversion is an inner transformation by which we are born into a new level of consciousness that leads us in new life directions. This does not happen through right thinking (as with Socrates) or through education (as with Confucius) or through enlightenment (as with Buddha). It happens through a surrender of self-centered willfulness in order to enter a personal faith relationship with God.

Conversion is both instantaneous and continuous. The title of one of the sermons in an 1897 revival service was "The First Step from Earth to Heaven." Conversion does have a first step, but it also has many other steps after that. Luther said that our old selves are drowned in baptism, but the old Adam is a mighty good swimmer. Conversion is a life-long process by which God continues to work changes in the way we feel, think, and act. An angry man stormed into a newspaper office, protesting that his name had been listed in the obituary column and this had damaged his business. The editor apologized, but the man was still angry. Finally, the editor said, "Okay, okay, I'll put your name in the birth column tomorrow and give you a fresh start." That is what happens in conversion. We make a fresh start. After that, conversion continues as long as we live.

Faith

Faith is a personal relationship with God. Just as love leads to thoughts of marriage, grace leads to faith. After we recognize and enter the kingdom of spiritual reality, we experience the feeling of grace (God's unlimited acceptance, forgiveness, and power for new life direction). This leads us to a faith relationship with God. Marriage has many different aspects (including rules, rituals, and morality), but marriage is primarily a relationship. So it is with faith: It is a personal relationship with a perfect partner.

The opposite of faith is not doubt but sin (self-centeredness). The opposite of sin (self-centeredness) is not virtue but faith. The moon has no light of its own. It can shine only when in the right relationship to the sun, the source of its reflected light. Faith is reflected light—a natural result of our moving into a personal relationship with God. Faith does not come through rules, rituals, or morality but by pointing our heart in a new direction.

Salvation

Salvation describes the new citizenship that results from grace, repentance, conversion, and faith. In conversion, we decide to cross the border into a new country. Salvation is our citizenship papers. Salvation is the wholeness of life that comes when we choose a relationship with God as a central focus.

Salvation is not a result of our efforts; it happens through our faith relationship with God. "For by grace you are saved through faith; and this is not your own doing, it is the gift of God—not because of works, lest any man should boast" (Eph. 2:8). We must decide to cross the border (repent), but we do not earn the citizenship papers. They are a gift of our faith relationship with God.

Distortions

The distortions of biblical Christianity's belief that we all need to repent take countless contemporary forms. These distortions look different from each other, but they all have three things in common: (a) all of them come from sin (self-centeredness); (b) all of them break the first commandment—"You shall have no other gods before me" (Exod. 20:3); and (c) all of them substitute something else for the need to turn away from self-centeredness and form a new relationship with God.

Secular universalism. In this view, nobody needs to repent. God, without our ever going to the bank, has already exchanged our currency. As one theologian who holds this view put it, "This is a God, without our ever going to the bank, has already exchanged our currency. As one theologian who holds this view put it, "This is a saved world!" On a *60 Minutes* show, Andy Rooney said that the media likes to make a big deal of people who win the lotteries. He said they ought to publish a list of the losers, too. The Bible says we would all be on that list: "All we like sheep have gone astray; we have turned everyone to his own way" (Isa. 53:6).

Ecclesiastical universalism. In this view, becoming a church member automatically puts us into a positive relationship with God. This is like the assumption that a marriage license can substitute for a marriage relationship.

Sin is an obsolete term. In this view, we have nothing of which to repent. Sin becomes an antique term that no longer has meaning in modern, educated society. A noted psychologist sums up this opinion by saying that the early Church told us to confess our sins to each other; the Roman Church told us to confess our sins to the priest; the Protestant Church told us to confess our sins to God; then, Freud told us that we have no sins to confess. This distortion is not, however, limited to contemporary culture. It was surely to counter a similar distortion that a New Testament writer said, "If we say we have no sin, we deceive ourselves, and the truth is not in us" (I John 1:8).

Sin is general rather than personal. In this view, sin becomes bad laws, racial prejudice, bad politics, bad politicians, communism, or the wrong political party in office. Sin becomes something that is wrong with society rather than something that is wrong with people. This distortion has in recent decades been prevalent among mainline church leaders. Communist reformer Karl Marx once accused Christianity of being the opiate of the people. For some Christians, political and social reform efforts have become an opiate of the Church.

Sin is immorality. In this view, clean living keeps us out of sin. If this were true, Jesus' conversation with the rich young ruler would have gone quite differently. This young man lived a moral and upright life. Yet, when Jesus asked him to make God the central focus of his life rather than other issues, he could not bring himself to do it.

Repentance has no moral implications. In this view, God loves us so much that he does not care what we do as long as we have at some point in life said we are sorry. As with a marriage relationship, biblical Christianity is more than morals and ethics, but it is not devoid of them.

Repentance can be done for us. The most common form of this distortion is the parent who sees to it that an infant is baptized but never involves that child in church life and Christian education.

Repentance has no discipleship implications. When Jesus healed Simon Peter's mother-in-law of a fever, she immediately got up and waited on them. That happens to everyone who is healed of wrong life directions through a God relationship. They begin to serve him in some way. If they do not, their healing is probably fake.

Self-salvation. In the many variations of this view, something we personally *do* brings us into a right relationship with God—joining a church, giving money, giving time, speaking in tongues, clear thinking, or having the right religious knowledge. Each of these is a modern form of the ancient do-it-yourself heresies. Each of them is like substituting some good thing we do for our spouse for a good relationship with our spouse. The initiative for bringing us into a positive relationship with God comes from his side of the equation (John 3:16). Christianity is not something we do. It is our response to something that has been done. We come to a relationship with God through faith (Eph. 2:8,9), not through some activity in which we engage (Rom. 4:5).

Church members are no longer sinners. In this view, the sinners are outside the church and the sinless are inside. Entering the church, if it is accomplished by a personal change of heart, makes us new people by putting us into a new relationship. It does not, however, make us perfect. Every conversion has its occasional reversion. We occasionally fall back into self-centered behavior—even though our primary focus is no longer self-centered. But being in the church does give us one big advantage: We are aware of our tendencies and far more inclined to seek God's help with them.

Someone said that rivers in the United States are so polluted that acid rain may make them cleaner. As we have seen from this list of distortions, that seems equally true of many contemporary beliefs about repentance. They are so polluted with ideas from other world religions and secular humanism that acid rain might improve them.

Going a New Direction

Repentance leads to a new relationship with God. In this new level of consciousness, God's priorities—loving others, and helping others find a transforming relationship with him—become our primary priorities. This replaces our old egocentric currency of loving ourselves, and saves us from futile efforts to find wholeness through self-love.

A young man belonged to a gang called the Midnight Auto Supply Company. They majored in stealing hubcaps at night. One evening an older man came to his street corner and started talking to the group about Jesus. The boy became angry and physically removed him from the corner. In the ensuing scuffle, the man handed him a tract. The unattractive mimeographed sheet contained a Bible verse, John 3:16. Three days later, while the boy was walking back from a gang meeting, he found the tract in his pocket. He looked at the verse and remembered that the man had told him to take "whosoever" out and put his own name in. He sat down in an empty lot and said, "If you are real and you love me, do something to change my life." God did. That boy is now president of Hospitality House, which serves a predominantly Black area of Minneapolis near North Side.[2]

How can we explain this experience rationally? We can't. We just know that this boy came to a point where he knew he had the wrong currency. He decided to ask God to exchange it. God did!

Discovery Questions for Group Study

1. List some ways (means of grace) by which you think God often helps people move toward repentance.

2. Ask everyone in the group who is willing to do so to share the way by which they first began moving toward repentance.

3. Do you agree or disagree with this chapter's definition of sin? Of grace? Of faith? Of conversion? Of salvation?

4. After looking at the list of ways in which people distort the concept of repentance, would you add other items to the list?

5. Which of the distortions of repentance do you think are most common in our community? Our denomination?

CHAPTER 9

IN GOOD COMPANY

A young woman, soon to graduate with a business degree, was being interviewed by the head hunters from various corporations who visited the campus every spring. As each one reviewed her grades and qualifications, she looked at the company's employment benefits. One interviewer, sensing that she was not as impressed as most graduates with the corporate salary scale and perks, said, "What exactly are you looking for in an employer?"

"The same thing I looked for in a marriage partner," she said, "a relationship that has dependable integrity. Money and benefits are important but not primary. I am more interested in the reputation a company has for treating its employees. I want something more than just working for a good company; I want to feel like I am in good company."

The faith relationship that develops after we enter God's kingdom of spiritual reality is somewhat like the relationship we establish with an employer who has dependable integrity. A faith relationship does not guarantee what will happen to us at every step of our journey through life, but it does guarantee that we are in good company. Nehemiah was not sure of his destiny when he left his secure position in the Babylonian court to go home and rebuild Jerusalem, but he was sure of his company. Paul was not sure what would happen to him when he became a traveling ambassador for Jesus Christ, but he knew in whom he believed. Faith is the relationship bond that connects each of us with the moving energy of God. *Biblical Christianity is, therefore, faith-centered.*

The Bible defines faith as "the assurance of things hoped for, the conviction of things not seen" (Hebrews 11:1). The clearest definitions of faith are not, however, found in statements like that but in the biographies of great Christians. As we see Paul, David Livingston, and John Wesley living out their response to God's calling, we see what faith is like. As we see them thinking and preaching and teaching their way toward a greater understanding of God, we gain our greatest understanding of what faith is.

Company Benefits

Faith produces two general benefits in human personality: Faith is an anxiety reducer that changes our feelings, and faith is a mountain mover that changes our circumstances.

Anxiety reducer: We all wish we could find a place to hide from fear and anxiety. That is impossible. To be alive means processing some frightening information. When x-rays pass through our body, they give physicians healing insights. But, if we held onto these x-rays, they could hurt us. Frightening pieces of information are like that. As they pass through our minds, they can inform and help us. If we hold that scary data in our minds too long, it injures us. Faith enables us to let go of these informational anxiety producers.

Mountain mover: Jesus asked some blind men if they believed he could heal them. They said yes. "According to your faith be it done to you," Jesus said (Matt. 9:29). While training his disciples, Jesus said, "he who believes in me will also do the works that I do; and greater works than these will he do" (John 14:12).

Scientists have identified a powerful plant growth hormone called brassinolide. In quantities of less than one-billionth of an ounce, it can double the size of plants. Our faith relationship with God, though as small as a mustard seed (or one-billionth of an ounce of brassinolide), can expand to move mountainous circumstances.

Signing On with Good Company

How do we develop a faith relationship with God powerful enough to change our feelings and our circumstances? In four ways.

Hearing: "Faith comes by hearing and hearing by the word of God" (Rom. 10:17).

Reading: This visual form of hearing can have the same result.

Stories about the continuing effectiveness of this method power the Gideons' work of placing Bibles in motel rooms. At moments of crisis, the words of these pages often become bricks with which God builds towers of faith.

Praying: Adult human nature is a disbelieving nature. We are more inclined to doubt than to believe. Prayer lets God's Holy Spirit come into our mind and power us toward faith.

Acting: An old legend says that when the Israelites, pursued by the Egyptian Army, came to the Red Sea, nothing happened until the first man waded in. Strong faith does not come from solitary thinking but from repeatedly taking action and experiencing the results, from wading in. Faith is not just believing something regardless of the evidence. Faith is daring to do something regardless of the consequence. Expecting a strong faith relationship to happen without acting is like expecting to get a pilot's license without risking the solo flight.

Distortions of Faith

Contemporary distortions of a personal faith relationship with God include the following:

Faith in a set of doctrinal beliefs. We see this distortion in every denomination and at every point on the theological spectrum. Saying biblical Christianity is a set of ideas is like saying marriage is a set of ideas.

Faith in our intellectual concepts regarding God. Most often seen in highly educated theologians and well-educated persons of liberal theological persuasion, this distortion occasionally appears among conservatives whose primary conviction is that they "really know the Bible." If strong faith were a matter of intellectual thought patterns, the most intelligent people would find it easier to relate to God, and children could not do it at all.

Faith in our emotional experiences with religion. Found most commonly in Charismatic-oriented Christians, this distortion is also seen in the person who at some point early in life had a great spiritual or conversion experience. Although these persons have not been to church in years, they may see themselves as Christians because of that one experience.

Faith in faith. This distortion is seen in persons who make positive thinking their faith rather than seeing positive thinking as one powerful aspect of Christian faith.

Faith in religion. This distortion is seen in the secular "Americans are religious because they are Americans" group. They believe in God, country, and Mother's Day in a firm and general way but know nothing of a personal faith relationship. They are Christians in the same way that they are Americans—by inheritance rather than by personal choosing.

Faith in good works. This heresy, practiced by the Roman Catholic Church of the 1500s through the sale of indulgences, launched the Protestant Reformation. It is still around, having reappeared in Protestantism in all kinds of disguises, like intellectual good works (think the right ideas and you are a true Christian) and emotional good works (have the right emotional experiences and you are a true Christian).

Faith without Christ. Biblical Christianity is not pluralistic but singularistic. It does not recommend belief in everything but belief in Jesus Christ. "No man comes to the Father, but by me" (John 14:6), is as strong, narrow, and intolerant as saying two times two makes four. While we may not totally understand Jesus' pronouncement (which seems to exclude some of our friends in other world religions) biblical faith is that narrow.

Faith in the Church. This distortion is like developing a personal relationship with the institution of marriage but never getting married.

Faith without discipleship. Faith that is nothing but good works is like a spouse who sends money home but never shows up in person. Faith that lacks works is like the spouse who says, "I love you," but never lifts a finger to demonstrate it. Both kinds of thinking are equally fake.

Faith in an absent God. This distortion is seen in people who believe in the idea of God but see him as an absentee landlord.

Faith in ritual. This distortion is seen in every denomination from the highest of high churches to the most casual of low churches. In its high church form, the rituals are candles and systematic priestly ceremony. In its low church form, the rituals include certain words and phrases (like "Jesus saves") repeated in prayers and preaching.

Too little faith. The distortion of faith that Jesus most frequently criticized was not a lack of faith but insufficient faith. "O ye of little faith" (Matt. 6:30; 8:26; 14:30-31; 16:8). In some ways, water in the gas tank is more dangerous than an empty tank: You have the impression that you will arrive at your destination. A totally empty tank is easier to recognize and fix.

How does one evade these and other distortions of faith? With great difficulty, and with hearing, reading, praying, and acting. Remove these four means of building and maintaining your personal faith relationship with God, and you slide into a distortion as naturally as uncautious drivers slide their cars off highways in ice storms.

Hialeah Faith

While Jimmy Carter was president, he told about the large number of strangers who appeared in the congregation he attended. He said that he hesitated to describe this as "worshiping with us." It was really more like visiting. Some of the visitors had not been in church often, but the congregation was pleased to make room for them. One Sunday, two tourists from Miami were in the service. Afterward, one turned to the other and said, "How did I do in the service?"

The other fellow said, "Well, you did okay, but the word is hallelujah, not Hialeah."[1]

How easily we develop a Hialeah faith while thinking we have hallelujah faith. Hallelujah faith is faith firmly grounded in hearing, reading, praying, and acting. Hialeah faith, on the other hand, is a skeleton of faith that is characterized by a lack of familiarity with God and his community. One gives us a relationship of dependable integrity. The other puts us in bad company.

Discovery Questions for Group Study

1. Do you think faith brings other benefits besides anxiety reduction and circumstance improvement?

2. Can you think of other ways by which we develop a strong faith relationship besides hearing, reading, praying, and acting?

3. Ask those in the group who are willing to share the ways they feel have been the most helpful to them in developing a strong faith relationship.

4. Are there other items that you feel belong on the list of faith distortions?

5. Which of the faith relationship distortions do you think is most common in our society? Our denomination?

CHAPTER 10

EXPERIENCE IS THE BEST STUDENT

John Wesley, reacting against the stale formalism of English church life, said that personal experience is a key element in what he called scriptural Christianity. The passage of two centuries has not diminished the accuracy of Wesley's observation.

The hub of biblical Christianity is God, Jesus Christ, and the Holy Spirit. The spokes by which human personality connects with that hub are recognition of spiritual reality, studying the Bible, prayer, and reason. The wheel (which in this analogy is the impact that biblical Christianity has on human personality) has six interlocking parts that fit together in an endless circle: Repentance is part of our rational response to connecting with God. Repentance leads to the strengthening of our personal faith relationship with God. Our faith relationship leads to a more and more personal experience with God. These personal experiences with God increase our trust in God. Our trust in God increases our feelings of hope. The more hopeful we are, the more joy we have. In the years after we initially connect with God, this six-part cycle repeats itself again and again, like the endless rolling of a wheel. The result is spiritual growth and maturity.

Remove the personal experience section from this six-part wheel of biblical Christianity, and it falls apart. Paul said, "Therefore, if any one is in Christ, he is a new creation; the old has passed away, behold, the new has come" (II Cor. 5:17). If we are not a new creation after connecting with God, our faith relationship has not been experienced, only intellectualized. Thinking about faith does not mean we have entered a faith relationship with God—any more than thinking about buying a new car means we own one. *Biblical Christianity is, therefore, personal experience-centered.*

A Two-House Legislature

Some theologians have thrown the authority of the Bible overboard by saying that personal experience is the ultimate authority for Christian faith. These "existentialist" theologians are, however, one-half accurate. As a law does not become law until ratified by both houses of Congress, biblical truth does not become truth for us until ratified in our own personal experience. Until that happens, it stays "in committee."

Distortions of Personal Experience

The spiritual experience of our parents can become a substitute for personal experience with God. This is especially obvious in people who will not transfer their church membership away from the old home church but will not formally affiliate with a congregation of that denomination in their present community.

Emotional feelings from the past can become a substitute for personal experience with God. A few people look back at some high moment in childhood or in a church camp where they felt very close to God and long for a rerun of that feeling. They refuse, however, to take any actions that would recreate these feelings in the present. This is a little like the person who longs to bring back the feelings of romance from dating days but refuses to take any of the actions that make for a meaningful marriage.

The various religious doctrines promoted by different denominational families have value. For some people, however, they become distorted substitutions for a personal experience with God.

Philosophical concepts and religious rituals of every type (including the various modes of baptism) can also block us from personal experience with God. Originally designed to connect us with God without personal experience, they can become substitutes for our connection with God.

Running from God

We often hear the Bible referred to as a record of "man's search for God." A pastor says that he thinks the reverse is more accurate:

the Bible is a record of people trying to avoid encounters with God. He may be right. People do not run away from the "idea" of God. Studies repeatedly indicate that more than nine out of ten Americans believe God exists. What we run from is not the idea of God but personal experience with God.

Francis Thompson wrote a poem, "The Hound of Heaven," in which he told of his years of running—and the ways in which God persistently tracked and hounded him through life, until he finally turned and embraced God. That happens to different people in different ways. Until it happens in some way, biblical Christianity cannot become real for us. The Bible is the best teacher, but without experience it has no students.

Discovery Questions for Group Study

1. Ask those in the group who are willing to share ways in which their own faith journey confirms the importance of personal experience in connecting with God.

2. Are there points at which you would disagree with the emphasis this chapter places on personal experience?

3. In what other ways do you think people try to make substitutions for personal experience in connecting with God?

4. To which of the distortions of personal experience do you think people in our culture are most prone? In our denomination?

5. What parts of our congregation's program are most helpful in strengthening your personal experience with God? Can you think of additional ideas for strengthening this aspect of our congregation's ministry that our leaders might want to consider?

CHAPTER 11

GOD'S SECURITY SYSTEM

In the early days of air travel, an eighty-year-old farmer took his first airplane ride at a county fair. After a ten-minute tour of the countryside, the plane landed. "How did you like it, Grandpa?" someone asked.

"Fine," the old farmer replied, "but I never did put my full weight down on the thing!" Many people, if asked to honestly describe how they handle the anxiety-producing ups and down of daily living, would say the same thing. They do not trust life enough to put their full weight down on it. Why is that? Differences in genetic and psychological makeup explain some of the differences in how people handle stress and anxiety. Several of the frequently prescribed anxiety-reducing methods—like exercise, deep breathing, and meditation—can help greatly. Optimism is also an important trait to cultivate. We should practice positive thinking until it becomes second nature to us. More than any other single factor, however, our ability to handle anxiety stems from our level of trust in God. The most powerful security system available to us is not what we can do for ourselves, but what we feel God is doing for us.

Although often used as if they were interchangeable terms, trust and faith are not the same. Trust is one of faith's several byproducts. Faith is the relationship we have with God on the journey of life. Trust is the confidence that, because of our faith relationship with God, what happens on each day of the journey will be in our best interest. Jesus described trust this way: "Therefore do not be anxious, saying, 'What shall we eat?' or 'What shall we drink?' or 'What shall we wear?'. . . . But seek first his kingdom and his righteousness, and all these things shall be yours as well (Matt. 6:31, 33). Paul described trust this way: "We know that in everything God works for good with those who love him, who are called according to his purpose" (Rom. 8:28). *Biblical Christianity is, therefore, trust-centered.*

Chronic worry is more than a bad habit. It denies the accuracy of Jesus' teaching regarding how God relates to people who relate to him in faith: "Are not two sparrows sold for a penny? And not one of them will fall to the ground without your Father's will. . . . Fear not, therefore; you are of more value than many sparrows" (Matt. 10:29, 31). Chronic worry denies the Gospel, the shortest meaning of which is, "Emmanuel . . . God with us" (Matt. 1:23).

When Australian pastor H.B. Macartney visited the pioneer China missionary, Hudson Taylor, he was amazed at Taylor's serenity in the face of a stressful schedule. When Macartney asked for the secret, Taylor said, "I could not possibly get through the work I have to do without the peace of God which passes all understanding keeping my heart and mind." Macartney later wrote, "He was in God all the time, and God was in him. It was the true abiding spoken of in John 15."[1] This is what Jesus meant when he said, "Do not be anxious" (Matt. 10:19). He was not advising optimism but the strong faith relationship with God that produces trust—the most powerful anti-anxiety weapon in the world.

Strengthening Trust

We cannot self-generate a feeling of trust; it grows out of our faith relationship with God. And yet, four personal attributes contribute to the degree of trust we experience.

Doing God's will: A chaplain tells about the special service he held at a veteran's hospital shortly after World War II. In his bombastic style of delivery, he cried out at one point in the sermon, "Why are we here? Why are we here?"

A patient from the psychiatric ward jumped up and yelled back, "We are here, brother, because we are not all there!" People are sometimes here in a lack of trust because they are not all there in doing God's will for their lives. Paul does not promise a feeling of trust to everyone, only to those who love God and cooperate in his purposes (Rom. 8:28). If our boat is moving against the wind of God's will, he cannot give us a feeling of confident trust.

Years of experience: The longer we know someone, the more experience we have in the relationship. If these experiences prove positive and dependable, trust grows. C.H. Spurgeon warned people not to imagine that a God who has helped them in six troubles will leave them in the seventh.[2] But without six experiences, we find that doubt surfaces more naturally than trust.

The attitude of acceptance: The caption on a poster says, "Life is something that happens while you are planning something else." The habit of either fighting or accepting these unexpected appointments with new directions greatly influences whether our faith relationship can develop great levels of trust. Years ago, the *Wall Street Journal* carried a story about Sally, an anxiety-prone teenager. Early one fall, while the leaves were still on the trees, Sally was riding with her grandfather after an exceptionally heavy snowstorm. He pointed out the difference between the elm trees and the pines. The elm branches were broken, but the evergreens were not. He told her that the elm branches broke because the tree held them rigid under the mounting weight of snow. By contrast, the evergreen, as its limbs become weighted, relaxes, lowers its branches, and lets the burden slip away. "Be a pine tree, granddaughter," he advised.[3] Trust is a byproduct of faith, but cultivating the attitude of acceptance increases our trust level.

The conviction that God can use bad experiences in good ways: Deaf actress Marlee Matlin won an Academy Award for her role in the movie *Children of a Lesser God.* When asked whether she believed in a God who would allow an eighteen-month-old baby to become deaf, she replied in sign language: "Yes, I believe in a greater being and a God that answers prayers, maybe not every prayer. Because if I hadn't lost my hearing, I wouldn't be talking to you now. I wouldn't be going to the Academy Awards. . . ."[4]

This does not mean that every tragic accident is an act of God, or that every bad thing that happens is good. Many bad things happen from ignorance and negligence. But everything bad contains the potential of a hidden good. People who diligently seek that good often make bad events work for them rather than against them.

They often turn disappointments into appointments with providential positives.

Distortions of Trust

The manner in which we can distort trust in biblical Christianity takes two general shapes. The first is easy to see because it is some form of idolatry. In primitive cultures, people trust idols made of stone, wood, and metal. In developed nations, idolatry is more sophisticated. There, people sometimes trust in money as their primary source of security—or their rational thinking ability, or science. The religious people in developed countries sometimes trust in the traditions, doctrines, and rituals of their church or denomination.

The second general kind of trust distortion is far less obvious and far more dangerous. We might call this distortion "trust in trust." Because psychology and psychiatry have increased our awareness of the powerful way that attitudes influence our lives, we easily fall prey to an over-concentration on that conviction. In this form of idolatry, encouraging people to develop the habit of a trusting attitude can substitute for the genuine trust generated by a faith relationship with God. Trust is not a self-developed personality quality that we can create in the same way that we knit a sweater. Trust comes from faith. Without a genuine faith relationship, any security blanket of self-talk quickly wears into a meaningless rag.

The Only Real Security

The kind of total security all of us are looking for is not really available. To obtain that, we would have to stay out of automobiles, because 20 percent of all fatal accidents happen there. We would need to avoid staying home, because 17 percent of all accidents occur there. Walking on streets and sidewalks accounts for another 14 percent of accidents. Air, rail, and boat travel generate 16 percent of all accidents.[5] Being alive anywhere, any time, in any circumstances always involves some danger.

Trust is the only answer to life in an undependable world—but not just any kind of trust will work. In Hamilton, Ontario, city workers were trimming tree limbs along the streets. Finding a nest of baby robins on a limb marked for trimming, they decided to leave it until the young birds were big enough to fly away. Several weeks later, they removed the limb. In the bottom of the nest, soiled and ragged, was a scrap of paper the mother robin had picked up as building material. On it these words were printed: "We trust in the Lord our God."[6] Jesus said this kind of trust is the only effective antidote against fear and anxiety.

Discovery Questions for Group Study

1. Do you agree or disagree with the idea that trust is a feeling derived from our faith relationship with God?

2. In addition to our faith relationship with God, are there factors that you think influence the development of trust in human personality?

3. Ask everyone in the group who is willing to share experiences and ideas that have helped them to develop greater levels of trust.

4. Are there other distortions of trust that you think should be added to the list in this chapter?

5. Which of the distortions of trust listed in this chapter do you think are most common in our community? Our denomination?

CHAPTER 12

THE CURE FOR FUTURE TENSE

Musician Skitch Henderson once commented that piano players have an old saying that goes like this: "If you can play 'Melancholy Baby,' you will always get a job." The chairman of the board of AT&T says that the same is true for speakers: "If you insist that the world is falling apart, you'll always get a podium."[1]

The accuracy of both comments relies on an emotional state which all of us, at times, feel—low spirits. Anyone who offers people a cure for that condition will likewise get a wide hearing. This accounts for the enormous sales of self-help books and for the success of much modern advertising in convincing us that we need something new. The best cure for low spirits is hope for a brighter future, and people who provide it will always have a job.

Christianity has been expanding for twenty centuries. Its adherents now number 33 percent of the world's 5.1 billion people. As might be expected of any movement with this kind of success record, Christian faith provides hope for despairing circumstances. Jesus described a vision of new life in a new world that includes new possibilities for family, friendships, and fellowship in a "new Israel." Paul extended this vision by proclaiming the Church the Body of Christ. Peter said we are "living stones" in this new future. The Book of Hebrews sees a new heaven and earth, a holy city. John says in the Book of Revelation that no matter how lost the game looks, Christians will win during overtime.

The Bible is a hope factory whose product meets the need of everyone in society—the poor, the enslaved, the demon-possessed, the lost, the lonely, the wounded, the exploited, the alienated, the wealthy, the prejudiced. There is hope for all. Yogi Berra said, "It ain't over 'til it's over." Biblical Christianity says the same thing:

Those who enter a faith relationship with God can have a new beginning. People who have faith develop trust, and people who trust have hope. *Biblical Christianity is, therefore, hope-centered.*

A Powerful Medicine

Hope is among the world's strongest preventative medications. Remove it and people die. A South African physician witnessed six cases of middle-aged Bantu men who died after being told, "You will die at sunset." Autopsy failed to show a cause of death. The victims, who believed the prophetic curse they received, felt helpless to do anything about it, became passive, depressed, gave up, and died.[2]

Doctors and chaplains who work with people on the outer edge of life often see them delay their own deaths through hope generated by the approach of a significant event. One study revealed that 46 percent of a random sample of people died in the first three months after their birthday, while only 8 percent died in the three months before their birthday. Other research indicates an unexplainable decrease in deaths before presidential elections and, in Jewish people, before Yom Kippur (the day of atonement).[3]

Hope is a powerful shaper of the world's reality. The president of Remington Freight Lines, Floyd Legler, says that people who are too reality-centered do not get much done. "People who are hope-centered get things done," he says. "If you are too reality-centered, you will be too limited by what you think cannot happen. What we focus on the most determines our results."

A Spiritually Manufactured Medicine

Short-term hope can be generated in many ways—through laughter, through the hearing of good news, through sharing your troubles with a friend, through reading books on positive thinking, through association with optimistic people, through a positive life experience. Deep and lasting hope, however, comes from the spiritual wells of our faith relationship with God. When Paul urges the Roman Christians to "abound in hope'" he is not prescribing a psychological medication but a theological one. "May the God of hope fill you with all joy and peace in believing, so that by the power of the Holy Spirit you may abound in hope," he says (Rom. 15:13).

A Proven Medicine

The deepest, most lasting hope is not based on circumstances, attitudes, or psychological therapies but on Christ. A tiny speck of land 2,000 miles west of Chile was named Easter Island by a Dutch navigator on Easter Day, 1722. For the person who forms a spiritual relationship with God, Easter is not a place to visit one day each year. Easter Island is a permanent residence. Christ was not just an optimist who advocated positive thinking. He proved that we live in a universe of spiritual reality more powerful than anything we can see with our eyes. He did this, not through his teachings or his sacrificial death on the cross but through his empty tomb.

Little Janie was saying her bedtime prayers. "Now I lay me down to sleep, I pray Thee, Lord, my soul to keep. If I should die before I wake. . . ." She stopped for a moment, then added, "Lord, if I die tonight, let's have breakfast together."[4] Janie's prayer is based on Easter, the ultimate proof of Christian hope's dependability. A God who has the power to empty tombs can do anything.

Distortions of Hope

Distortions of hope take two general forms: One is the habit of chronic pessimism and worry. An old story tells about a motorist who got stuck in the mud on a country road. A farmer came along and pulled him out, but only after saying it would cost thirty dollars. The incensed driver got back into the car and said to his wife, "Don't worry. I'll make him earn every cent of it. I'll keep my brakes on!"[5] That is the way some people move forward all their lives—with their brakes on. This habit is a straightforward denial of God's presence and power.

Feelings of hopelessness and despair are sinful. Permitting ourselves to be taken prisoner by depression denies the power of God to help us adjust to or move our mountainous circumstances. When we fall into hopelessness, we fall into hell—a place so disconnected from God that he can no longer help us. A tombstone in Erie, Pennsylvania, says, "Why live and be miserable when for a few dollars and sales tax you can rest here?" That statement, if it is a true reflection of the individual's opinion who is buried there, is the opposite of biblical Christianity. He or she had already entered hell before departure from life. Such a view denies the gospel—"God with us." It assumes that God is either dead or asleep, unable to help us break through to a meaningful life.

The second general way that we can distort hope is by trying to manufacture it ourselves. A man suffering from intense depression was about to jump from the Brooklyn Bridge when a policeman stopped him. In the conversation that followed, the man said his life was hopeless and begged the officer to let him jump. The policeman made a deal with him. He would listen for five minutes to the man's reasons why life was not worth living. Then, the man would listen for five minutes as the policeman told him why life was worth living. After that, if the man still wanted to jump, the policeman would not stop him. According to the story, the man took his five minutes. The officer took his five minutes. Then they joined hands and jumped off the bridge. Any kind of hope that we can manufacture ourselves can be unmanufactured by ourselves. Genuine hope is not something people can be argued into or out of. It is a gift that comes as a result of our faith relationship with God.

A Happy Ending

The depth of contemporary despair and the resulting need for hope are reflected in the incredible growth of the humor industry in the United States. In the past five years, the number of comedy clubs has grown from 15 to more than 300. The Professional Comedians Association says that the number of professional comics has increased from a few hundred to more than 5,000.[6]

A little boy had been promised a new puppy for his birthday, but he had a tough time choosing among the candidates at the pet shop. He finally decided on a shaggy pup of questionable parentage that was wagging his tail furiously. When Dad asked why he wanted that one the boy said, "I want the one with the happy ending." All of us want and need to see a happy ending in our future. That happens through hope. Genuine hope happens, not by attending a comedy club, but by a faith relationship with God.

Discovery Questions for Group Study

1. Ask group members to share reasons why they think the amount of depression and what appears to be a resulting interest in humor have increased among people in our society.

2. Do you agree or disagree with the statement that we cannot manufacture hope by ourselves? Why?

3. Do you agree or disagree with the statement that chronic worry is a sin? Why?

4. Do you agree or disagree with the statement that hell is hopelessness? Why?

5. Ask group members who are willing to share ways in which they find their hope strengthened when facing difficult circumstances.

CHAPTER 13

BETTER THAN HAPPINESS

A student pastor in the 1950s served two small congregations. After preaching at 8:30 A.M., he drove fifteen miles to preach at the other church during their 11:00 A.M. service. The first congregation was smaller and consisted mostly of older persons. The service in the second congregation was attended by mostly young adults with children. Immediately, he began to notice radically different response patterns from the two groups. The older members in the first congregation seldom permitted themselves to smile at the bits of humor in his sermon. When he preached the same message to the second congregation, they laughed uproariously at these points. As the young pastor grew more experienced, he realized that the older Christians in that denomination had grown up during a time when having fun in church was considered inappropriate.

Every era contains some illogical thinking patterns that are easily recognized from a historical distance. Today, few Christians would label fun off limits in church life. Not only is joy seen as appropriate, but it is also viewed as a logical characteristic of persons who enter a strong faith relationship with God. Jesus said, "These things I have spoken to you, that my joy may be in you, and that your joy may be full" (John 15:11). Faith and trust produce hope, and hope generates joy. A Christian faith without joy would hardly be classified as *Christian* faith. *Biblical Christianity is, therefore, joy-centered.*

Happiness Is Not Joy

Happiness depends mostly on happenings. Joy is deeper and different. Happiness comes from circumstances. Joy is an attitudinal state that changing circumstances cannot control. We can be *happy* in good circumstances but not in bad ones. By contrast, the *joy* that stems from faith, trust, and hope can survive in the dry, rocky soil of difficulty. "With all our affliction, I am overjoyed" (II Cor. 7:4), Paul writes to the Corinthian Church. On another occasion, when he and Barnabas were effective in making converts but were driven out of that district by persecution, Paul says, "And the disciples were filled with joy and with the Holy Spirit" (Acts 13:52).

A contemporary writer describes joy with the analogy of a small fishing boat on Puget Sound. It bobs in high tide, rests on the rocks at low tide, and the storm winds sometimes pull it violently. It is not free from distress, but it is held secure by its anchorage to an immovable rock.[1] Joy is different from the happiness that comes from positive events. Those who have happiness are lucky. Those who have joy are anchored to a rock that keeps them blessed.

Serving Enhances Joy

Christian discipleship does not produce joy; rather, our faith, trust, and hope produce joy. Christian service does, however, enlarge the joy that the Holy Spirit gives through our faith relationship (Galatians 5:22). God is by nature caring, and we are made in his image. When we try to care for people in active ways, we are like a turned on light bulb. Our outer behavior is congruent with our inner design and purpose, and we shine with joy.

Distortions of Joy

Most of the ways we distort the concept of joy come from the same root cause: trying to have joy without having a faith relationship with God and living out the natural result of that—self-giving love toward other people. This does not mean that we can generate Christian joy by working harder at helping people. But joy goes with loving God and serving others like a light bulb goes with a socket. All our efforts to manufacture joy by other means are as hopeless as trying to get light by holding the bulb in your hand and blowing on it.

Captives of Joy

In Agua de Dios, a town in Colombia, South America, the central plaza features the life-size statue of a man playing a piano. His face carries a broad smile. A nameplate identifies the pianist as Luis A. Calvo, who wrote several of Colombia's favorite songs. This town was once a leper colony where barbed wire barriers kept captive persons who were slowly dying. Calvo, a leper, died of his terrible disease there. Why does the statue show him smiling as he sings and plays? Because he was captured by something stronger than barbed wire—the same thing that captured the Apostle Paul—the joy that springs eternal from the hope that comes from trust that comes from a faith relationship with God.

Discovery Questions for Group Study

1. Do you agree or disagree with this chapter's assertion that happiness is related to our life circumstances and joy is related to our faith relationship? Why?

2. Do you think factors other than our faith relationship and our discipleship influence the level of our joy?

3. Do you know Christians who seem to give themselves in service yet do not seem joyful? If so, how would you explain this behavior?

4. Are there other ways that you think we can distort the concept of Christian joy besides the one cited in this chapter?

5. Ask those in the group who feel comfortable in doing so to describe the most joyful Christian they have known.

PART IV

THE WHEELBARROW

*HOW BIBLICAL CHRISTIANITY
INFLUENCES OUR SOCIETY
AND WORLD*

CHAPTER 14

DISCIPLESHIP

The only visible result during one week of evangelistic preaching in a Scottish church came at the final service. One little boy came forward during the invitation. The pastor felt disheartened at this light response to a heavy effort. He did not, however, realize what had happened. Through that boy, the entire African continent was opened to Christianity and modern civilization. His name was David Livingstone.[1]

This story illustrates the chief manner by which biblical Christianity impacts the world. It happens through people who, one at a time, make a life-changing connection with God. These persons, individually and collectively, are the wheelbarrow by which God carries positive change to human society. The hub of biblical Christianity is God, Jesus Christ, and the Holy Spirit. The spokes by which persons connect with that hub are experience with spiritual reality, the Bible, prayer, and reason. The wheel by which biblical Christianity influences human personality is repentance, faith, personal experience, trust, hope, and joy. The wheelbarrow by which biblical Christianity influences society is discipleship, love, forgiveness, meeting needs, tolerance, and freedom.

Although the Greek word for disciple, *mathetes*, is used 259 times in the New Testament, discipleship is among the most misunderstood of nouns. Becoming a disciple is not like joining a fan club. A fan can admire the hero or heroine from a distance without making any personal behavior change. A disciple, on the other hand, tries to become like the admired person. *Biblical Christianity is discipleship-centered.* A disciple is a follower, not a fan. If our Christ-connection is not making us Christ-like, it is something other than biblical Christianity.

Many contemporary definitions of discipleship are long and complicated. A Gallup Survey, for example, says that Americans are most likely to define being a follower of Jesus as "obeying the Ten Commandments, forgiving those who have wronged you, putting others' needs before your own, and living in such a way as to draw others to Christ."[2] Jesus, however, usually defines discipleship in two words—"follow me"—or in one short sentence: "If any man would come after me, let him deny himself and take up his cross and follow me" (Matt. 16:24). Jorge Himitian is following Jesus' pattern of simplicity when he says that "A disciple is one who believes everything that Christ says and is disposed to do everything that Christ commands."[3] John Wesley used the same short-form definition by saying that the goal of the Christian life is to "have the mind of Christ and walk as he walked."[4] However you choose to define it, being a follower comes down to two things: thinking like Jesus thought and acting like Jesus acted.

Thinking Like Jesus Thought

How did Jesus think? He summarized it in the Great Commandment—love God and neighbor. A woman in an underdeveloped country was, like all her friends, a victim of deep poverty. She became a Christian and wanted to show her love for God. Each day as she prepared rice for her family, she set aside one handful. Each week, she gave what she had saved to God. That is thinking like Jesus thought. A congregation in Perryton, Texas, borrowed $35,000 to renovate the faculty offices at the Phillips University Seminary in Enid, Oklahoma. The church did not have the money; they borrowed the money. That is thinking like Jesus thought.

Acting Like Jesus Acted

How did Jesus act? He helped, served, cared, healed, taught, preached, and sacrificed himself on a cross. We often define the word disciple as learner. That is technically accurate but functionally dangerous. Discipleship is more than cerebral learning; it involves action. Jesus said, "By this my Father is glorified, that you bear much fruit, and so prove to be my disciples" (John 15:8).

An old story tells of a young man who came to a pastor and said that he wanted to be a Christian. The pastor instructed him to read the Book of Acts as preparation for this important decision. Weeks passed, but the young man did not return. The pastor began to think he had made a serious mistake in his suggestion. Finally, almost a year later, the young man appeared at his study door. When the surprised pastor asked where he had been, the man said, "You told me to read the Book of Acts. Every time I started to read, it told me to do something. So, I stopped reading and went and did it. I have just been too busy to get back." That is acting like Jesus acted. His ideals did not stay home in his head. They went to work.

Distortions of Discipleship

The substitutions people make for genuine discipleship form an almost endless list, each of which is quite deceptive to its owners. Some examples are:

Substituting Doctrine for Discipleship. Flip Wilson is quoted as saying in response to a question about his denominational preference, "I am a Jehovah's spectator! I would be a witness but that would require too much commitment." Heart specialists tell us that when you become a spectator of sports rather than a participant, the wrong things go up and the wrong things go down. Cholesterol, triglycerides, heart rate, blood pressure, and body weight go up. Stamina, muscle strength, oxygen consumption, and thinking ability go down.[5] Faith without works is not just dead; it is deadly. Faith without action is less than faith.

Substituting Ritual for Discipleship. A minister on a dark street felt a gun in his back. When the robber saw the clerical collar, he withdrew his demand for money. "I'm sorry. I never take money from preachers."

The pastor relaxed and said, "Good, here, have a cigar."

The robber replied, "Thanks, anyway, but I don't smoke during Lent."

Substituting Morality for Discipleship. A professor in a small church college once described himself and his faculty colleagues like this: "We don't drink. We don't swear. We don't smoke. We don't dance. We don't play cards. But we have no important virtues."[6]

Substituting Family for Discipleship. When Jesus challenged the man who excused himself from becoming a disciple because he needed to attend a family funeral, he was not denigrating family life. Jesus was saying in this living parable that we should not substitute good things for the best thing.

Substituting Some Other Discipleship for Christian Discipleship. Everyone is a disciple of something. Everyone has a bulls eye in the target at which his or her life shoots. A man was walking down the street with a sandwich board strapped over his shoulders. The front side said, "I am a fool for Christ's sake." As he moved along, the sign on the back became visible: "Whose fool are you?"[7] If we are not a disciple of Jesus Christ, we are a disciple of something else. Whatever our beliefs, we are becoming images of them. There are no non-disciples, only various types of disciples.

Christ Sat for a Portrait

A young pastor visiting points of historical interest in San Antonio remarked about the portraits along the inside wall of the Alamo. Near the main entrance was a painting with this inscription, "James Butler Bonham—no picture of him exists. This portrait is of his nephew, Major James Bonham, deceased, who greatly resembled his uncle. It is placed here by the family that people may know the appearance of the man who died for freedom."[8]

Jesus did not sit for a portrait either. Or did he?

Discovery Questions for Group Study

1. Do you agree or disagree with defining discipleship as thinking and doing what Jesus thought and did? Why or why not?

2. Do you think items like attending church and giving money to

help do God's work should be added to this chapter's definition of discipleship?

3. What else would you like to add to the list of distortions of discipleship in this chapter?

4. Which distortions of discipleship do you think are most prevalent in our community? Our denomination?

5. Ask members of the group who are willing to share experiences in which they learned to tell the difference between discipleship and one of its distortions.

CHAPTER 15

WHAT GOD LOOKS LIKE

A pastor was serving as substitute teacher for the first and second graders during Vacation Bible School. After making the point that we are Jesus' hands and feet in today's world, he asked where they thought Jesus lives now. He got the expected answer—"Jesus lives inside us"—from all but one of the children. A little boy kept staring at his hands and feet with a puzzled expression. Looking at the huge picture of Jesus hanging on the wall, he said, "But I'm so little and Jesus is so big. How can he fit inside me?" The pastor explained that Jesus is Spirit, but the boy's continued resistance indicated that he did not fully grasp that concept. "If Jesus lives inside of me, why isn't he sticking out somewhere?" he asked.

The boy's question speaks a profound theological truth. If we connect with the hub of biblical Christianity—God, Jesus Christ, and the Holy Spirit—that experience will impact the world in some visible way. The Spirit of God living in Jesus showed in what he said and did. Likewise, when Jesus lives in us, he sticks out somewhere. If someone were to shoot a video of Jesus "sticking out" of us, love would be an obvious element in the picture. William Walwyn, an English agitator of the seventeenth century, said, "Show me thy faith by thy works. If faith works, it works by luve." Love is a major element of the wheelbarrow by which God carries the weight of the world's hurt. *Biblical Christianity is, therefore, love-centered.*

A Picture of the Picture

Love as Jesus defined it has three major characteristics:

Love is exemplified by the way Jesus loves us: "Love one another as I have loved you" (John 15:12). During the 1965 football season, Green Bay Packers' quarterback Bart Starr developed an incentive program to motivate his son toward better school work. For every perfect paper Bart junior brought home, Bart senior gave him ten cents. After an especially tough game in St. Louis, Starr returned home weary and dejected. He had played below his best, his body had been battered, and the trip home was long and tiring. But when he entered his bedroom late that night, he immediately felt better. Attached to his pillow was a note: "Dear Dad, I thought you played a great game. Love, Bart." Taped to the note were two dimes.[1] That is the way Jesus loved us. To love like Jesus loves means to love in spite of imperfections.

Love extends beyond our family and our church: "Love your neighbor as yourself" (Matt. 22:39). In his story of the Good Samaritan, Jesus makes clear his definition of the word *neighbor*: it includes people we do not know (Luke 10:25-37), especially the poor and hurting (Luke 14:12-14). A leading insurance company has a group of employees who claim to be "Good Hands People." Their advertisements show agents standing with hands out-stretched, palms upward, indicating that they will take care of you. When church people operate at optimum biblical Christianity standards, that would make a fitting ad for what they do.

Love extends to the people who hurt us: "Love your enemies" (Luke 6:35). Biblical Christianity is quite different from some of the other world religions on this point. Buddhist scripture, for example, says that we cannot defile or purify someone else. The Bible teaches the opposite. It says that Jesus raised each of us to new possibilities by becoming vulnerable on a cross. It says that if we are willing to reverse our instinctive reflex toward self-centeredness and become vulnerable by loving the people who hurt us, that action opens the possibility for them to change.

Love with these three characteristics is quite different from the sentimental and romantic love generally meant when people use the word. Anyone can love in the way that love is usually defined. The love defined in biblical Christianity is "in spite of" love. It takes action in spite of difficulties with others. Rather than giving them what we think they earn and deserve, it gives them more than we think they deserve. It acts toward other people the way God acted toward us when Jesus went to the cross.

Love Is a Gift

Does "in spite of" love for your enemies sound like superhuman behavior? It is. This kind of love cannot be self-manufactured. It comes only as a gift, and it comes from our faith connection with a power plant that transmits supernatural voltage. God does not merely urge us to love: he *is* love (I John 4:16). By connecting with him, we gain the power to love as he loves. That is why Jesus says loving God is the first and greatest commandment (Matt. 22:37-38). Without that power source, the second commandment to love neighbor as self is like trying to fly the Atlantic in a hang glider. This is surely why Jesus does not tell us to *understand* God. You can understand someone without loving them. If you love them, you are connected to them. Relationship with God, not knowledge about God, lets the power come through.

Exactly how this power line connects with us is not totally explainable by rational means. The process is a bit like the way a solar calculator works. Hold it in the sunlight, and invisible rays translate into complex calculations. In the dark, a solar calculator does not work. We are like a solar calculator when, without an outside power source, we try to love the people who hurt us. The ability to love like Jesus loved is a gift. We cannot make it; we can only receive it and pass it on.

Distortions of Love

Substituting the study of religious knowledge for the intended goal of religious knowledge, love. As John Wesley said, "Beware you be not swallowed up in books! An ounce of love is worth a pound of knowledge."[2]

Substituting the doctrines and authority systems of organized church life for the intended goal of church life, love. During the reign of Charles V, torture was legalized and used by the ruling princes. In the great Fortress Hohensalburg (overlooking the city of Salzburg, Austria, where *The Sound of Music* was filmed), one can still see the rooms where the "rack" and the "strappado" were used to extract confessions and execute sentences—sometimes with persons deemed to hold inappropriate religious beliefs. Only a few yards below the torture chamber was a small "house chapel" just off the elaborate living quarters provided for the ruling prince. Christians of every century are prone to worship the forms of their religion and practice the opposite of its spirit. How valiantly we often affirm the Lordship of him who said we should love one another—and then use much of our cerebral energy to hate and hurt each other. As the great New England preacher Henry Ward Beecher said, "Everyone has conscience enough to hate; few have religion enough to love."

Substituting discussions of love for the doing of love. In its report to a denominational board regarding work among American Indians, a committee said that the needs of Native Americans have been "overstudied." That describes a great deal of church activity. Northrop Frye, chancellor of Victoria University, Toronto, Canada, says that we often discuss the question of why God permits so much evil and suffering. Frye says a better question is, "Why do we permit so much evil and suffering?"[4] If we spent more time discussing this question, we would surely come closer to the doing of love.

The world watched in admiration as Henry Aaron hit his 715th home run, breaking Babe Ruth's remarkable record. When a newspaper reporter asked what was going on in his mind at that historical moment, Aaron said, "I don't remember the noise, or the two kids that ran on the field. My teammates at home plate, I remember seeing them. I remember my mother out there and she hugging me. That's what I'll remember more than anything about that home run when I think back on it. I don't know where she came from, but she was there." Holy Week carries a similar message. Through all the crowds of defeats and triumphs in life, a powerful love keeps reaching out to us. God does not sit at home in heaven, watching on TV to see how well we play the game. He came to be with us. In that action, he empowers us to sacrifice for others in the spirit of his love. If we do not do this, we are something other than biblical Christians.

Our Best Advice

In the movie *Oh, God!* George Burns, who plays God, appears in a final dramatic courtroom scene to lend credibility to his present-day prophet, John Denver, who plays a frightened supermarket manager. After a dazzling display of card tricks to prove to the judge that he is really God, Burns makes several theologically profound remarks. Then, in the final moments of the movie, he makes himself invisible and leaves the courtroom through the noisy, swinging doors that enclose the judge's bench. As we hear the final squeaks of the invisible departing shoes walking out through the great double doors in the back, he says, "Try not to hurt each other. There's been enough of that."

Biblical Christianity says the same thing but much more. "Love one another, as I have loved you" (John 15:12). When we do that, people can see what God looks like.

Discovery Questions for Group Study

1. Do you agree or disagree with the three characteristics of Christian love listed in this chapter?

2. Can you think of other characteristics of Christian love that should be added to this list?

3. Ask those in the group who are comfortable in doing so to describe the most loving person they have known and to say whether they feel that person's faith relationship with God was a major empowering aspect of that love.

4. Do you know people who exhibit the characteristics of Christian love but are not regular church attenders? If so, how do you explain this?

5. Can you think of other distortions of Christian love that should be added to the list in this chapter?

6. Which distortions of Christ's love do you think are most common in our community? Our denomination?

CHAPTER 16

LOVE IN WORK CLOTHES

An Islamic student from the Middle-East cheated on his midterm chemistry exam at a small Christian college in North Carolina. After a reprimand and brief suspension, he was readmitted. He did the same thing again at the end of the semester. In the interview during which the college president expelled him, the boy said, "You have to forgive me."

"What do you mean?" the president asked.

"This is a Christian college," he replied, "and your religion says you have to forgive me seventy times seven."

His manipulative appeal to stay in school failed, but the boy left the president in deep thought. The scripture he had alluded to was both crystal clear and incredibly confusing: "Then Peter came up and said to him, 'Lord, how often shall my brother sin against me, and I forgive him? As many as seven times?' Jesus said to him, 'I do not say to you seven times, but seventy times seven' " (Matt. 18:21-22).

That conversation in the president's office is, however, more the exception than the rule in everyday life. Most of the time, our difficulty is not so much in understanding whether Jesus' teaching about forgiveness applies to a specific situation. Our difficulty is in taking action in the situations where it clearly does apply. In his story of the Good Samaritan and his statement that we should love our enemies, Jesus defines who our neighbor is—everyone. In his statements about forgiveness, he tells us what love looks like when it puts on work clothes and does its toughest task among those neighbors. William Carlos Williams writes,

> What power has love but forgiveness?
> In other words
> by its intervention
> what has been done
> can be undone
> What good is it otherwise?[1]

God's love for us is called grace. God grants us his grace even though he sees that our lives sometimes go in the wrong directions and that we do not deserve forgiveness. Our love for other people, even though they have wronged us and do not deserve it, is called forgiveness. *Biblical Christianity is, therefore, forgiveness-centered.* Without forgiveness, love can remain a cerebral, sentimental word.

Essential But Difficult

Best-selling author Stephen King said in a writer's magazine, "Only God gets things right the first time."[2] That applies to life as much as to writing. We all need, at times, to receive forgiveness. Yet, when we turn forgiveness around and focus it on others, we find the "give" in forgiveness difficult to do. We have all experienced the joy and sense of relief that Dag Hammarskjöld described in his famous quote: "Forgiveness is the answer to the child's dream of a miracle by which what is broken is made whole again, what is soiled is made clean."[3] Yet, what happens when we find ourselves in a situation that calls for us to forgive people? Our love often has trouble getting its work clothes on and walking across the threshold from our minds into our relationships. Jesus says that God desires mercy, not sacrifice (Matt. 12:7). That means mercy to everyone, even those who neither deserve it nor are willing to give it in return. But that verse is harder to live than to quote. King Alfonso X of Spain said, "If I had been present at creation, I would have given some useful hints." One of these tips might have been to construct people with a greater innate disposition toward forgiving those who hurt them.

Essential and Spiritual

Jesus says that the quality of our forgiveness influences the quality of our faith relationship with God. "And whenever you stand praying, forgive, if you have anything against anyone" Jesus says, "so that your Father also who is in heaven may forgive you your trespasses" (Mark ll:25-26). Three elements—God's forgiveness of us, our sense of feeling forgiven, and our forgiveness of other people—are like three strands of a silken, braided cord. Cut the strand of our forgiveness of others, and the whole cord comes apart. And how easily and how often we break this strand of the spiritual cord. Two police magistrates were driving home one night when they were stopped by a motorcycle policeman. They were each given a citation. When their cases came up the next day, they agreed to take turns—with each hearing the other's case. The first pled guilty and was fined $20 and costs. When they changed places, the second magistrate was shocked to receive a fine of $50 plus costs. "Isn't that unfair?" he asked. "I only fined you $20."

"Yes," the other magistrate said, "but there is too much of this kind of thing going on. This is the second case we've had today."

Thomas Fuller said, "He that cannot forgive others breaks the bridge over which he must pass himself; for every man has need to be forgiven." Jesus said the same thing: "Judge not, and you will not be judged; condemn not, and you will not be condemned; forgive, and you will be forgiven" (Luke 6:37). Yet, we often do break that bridge, and thereby break our spiritual path to God. Spiritual growth, therefore, involves a continual rebuilding of that bridge.

Essential and Unnatural

Two mothers were talking. "How is John?" asked one mother, referring to the other's son, who had caused his mother much heartache and trouble. The mother shook her head and said sadly, "I'm afraid he just gets worse and worse."

"Well," said the friend, "if he were my son, I would tell him to leave."

"Yes," replied the mother, "and if he were your son, I would tell him to leave, too."

The kind of love and forgiveness described in this story is natural. Mother-to-child forgiveness is built into the relationship from birth. But the love with work clothes on that Jesus defines with the word *forgiveness* is not part of our natural, innate personality equipment. We must obtain it from outside ourselves. Someone defined forgiveness as the odor flowers give off when they are trampled upon, but the normal scent of human flowers when trampled on is more like skunk than roses.

Essential and Miraculous

How, then, is the wheelbarrow of forgiveness possible? Only through our faith relationship with God. Forgiveness, like love, is a gift. All the distortions of forgiveness tend, therefore, to originate in some kind of effort to manufacture by psychological and social means something that only God can give us.

William Blake said that the glory of Christianity is to conquer by forgiveness.[4] Paul says, "See that none of you repays evil for evil, but always seek to do good to one another and to all" (I Thess. 5:15). That kind of behavior can only happen by a miracle that God works in us. The full name of unconditional love is Jesus Christ. By connecting with him, we can receive the miraculous power to forgive. Apart from him, the cup of our human nature will very likely keep overflowing with its natural venom of anger and bitterness.

Albert Speer, Hitler's director of German economy, was sentenced to twenty years in Berlin's Spandau Prison. He experienced unexpected kindness from the Russian prison guards, whose country had suffered so much from the Nazi regime. The guards, Speer wrote, taught him that "all historical grandeur means less than a modest gesture of humanness; that all national honor . . . is insignificant compared to simple readiness to help others."[5] Jesus said the same. He not only said it; he did it: "Father, forgive them; for they know not what they do" (Luke 23:34). He not only did it; he gives us the power to do it.

Discovery Questions for Group Study

1. Can you think of instances when it is inappropriate to forgive people?
2. In what kind of circumstances do you find it the most difficult to forgive?
3. Do you know people who are not regular church attenders,

yet seem to be extremely forgiving by nature? If so, how do you explain this in the light of what this chapter says about forgiveness being a result of our faith relationship with God?

4. Someone has said that most first children and only children have had such high ideals and perfectionism instilled in them that they find it hard to forgive people. Do you agree or disagree with that opinion?

5. Ask group members who feel comfortable in doing so to share ways that they feel have helped them to replace bitterness with forgiveness.

CHAPTER 17

THE HEART OF WHAT MATTERS

Many people leave their television sets on all day during the Jerry Lewis Labor Day telethon. Many of these same people seldom watch television. The enormous financial success of this annual effort to fight muscular dystrophy stems from a widely agreed upon conviction: We should work together to heal hurts and help people live better lives.

Many of the beliefs held by people in our culture are the opposite of what Jesus taught. This one is identical. *Biblical Christianity is centered on human need.* Jesus said, "I am came that they might have life, and have it abundantly" (John 10:10). While they may sometimes disagree on a definition of the word *abundant,* Christians and non-Christians tend to agree that they want to experience a more abundant life and want to help others do so.

What are the basic human needs through which life becomes abundant? Abraham Maslow's famous hierarchy of needs is a widely accepted truism. Maslow says that we have physiological needs, safety needs, love and belonging needs, self-esteem needs, and self-actualization needs. But identifying those five basic needs does not mean we know how to achieve them. Biblical Christianity says that we achieve those five basic human needs (and help others to achieve them) in three ways: by connecting with God, by connecting with other people, and by connecting with great causes.

The God Connection

One of the most ironic elements in contemporary mainline church life is a neglect of the basic human need for a spiritual relationship with God. To compensate for this neglect of the spiritual, many new organizations have appeared during the past thirty years. Examples: Cursillo, the Charismatic Churches, Neighborhood Bible Studies, Campus Crusade. This phenomenon illustrates two obvious facts: people want to connect with God; and if churches do not help people connect with God, people will seek other ways to make that connection.

An Australian pastor tells about a lighthouse along a bleak coast. The lighthouse keeper was given enough oil for a month. During the next few days, several friends came by to borrow some oil. He gave a farmer some for his reading lamp, a woman some for a heating stove, and a mechanic some for an engine. A few days before the end of the month, the lighthouse lamp ran out of oil. Three ships crashed on the rocks that night and 100 people died. When charges of negligence were brought against the lighthouse keeper, his superiors told him that he had one task—to keep the light burning. The other things he did were fine gestures of helpfulness, but they were secondary. When Jesus said, "Go therefore and make disciples of all nations" (Matt. 28:19), he was not just building an organization; he was advocating the meeting of a basic human need—the need to connect with God. When churches neglect that need in favor of meeting other important needs, both the ships and the lighthouses fall into troubled waters.

The People Connection

Why do Gallup surveys show that Americans are more lonely than persons in many other nations?[1] The reasons are numerous. Because of geographic mobility, the three generations within our families are often disconnected from each other in ways not true in former decades. Almost 20 percent of Americans move each year. Thus, many of us are disconnected from familiar places. We get lost in the lonely crowds as we inhabit the rootless, changing cities which replaced the stable, rural towns of earlier decades. The high divorce rate accentuates this disconnection even more. Modern life also tends to disconnect us from the familiar causes on which we once agreed and scatters us among fragmented pressure groups that promote disagreement. Additionally, instead of relating to people, many of us relate to computer screens all day. For recreation, many of us are connected to headsets that feed in our own personalized choice of music. The much repeated philosophical ideal of "doing your own thing" has led many of us to become runaway individualists who are disconnected from everyone in every way. Small wonder that one of the most common statements heard in counseling offices is, "I don't feel connected."

Many aspects of our contemporary culture are conscious or unconscious efforts to reconnect with value systems. The phone company urges us to "reach out and touch someone." The rapid increase in the number of psychologists, psychiatrists, counselors, and other forms of "rent a friend" services is at least partially a response to this need. A billboard advertising a radio station in Atlanta, Georgia said, "Country Songs Are Stories"—and illustrated this principle with a song title: "Don't Kick My Tires If You Ain't Gonna Take Me for a Ride." The rising popularity of country music is at least partially a response to the disconnected feeling most Americans are suffering in this period of history: a story makes you feel connected to other people.

Biblical Christianity is still the world's best answer to this need. It connects us with a group of people who know our name, who pray for us, with whom we join in worship, and with whom we work to help and heal other people. People in our culture have ceased to be the indiscriminate "joiners" of community groups that they were in the 1950s. Now, they are looking for something deeper. They want to feel a sense of "belonging" rather than merely joining. Biblical Christianity meets that need, and all over the world young adults are rediscovering that ancient truth.

The Great Cause Connection

The passing parade of human needs provides an endless list of great causes that caring people want to address. If these needs are not met, countless people are either hurt or fail to reach their highest potential. Yet, meeting the needs of the indigent is only one-half of the need. When Paul quoted Jesus as saying, "It is more blessed to give than to receive" (Acts 20:35), he was telling us that much of life's meaning derives from reaching outside ourselves to help other people. Helping helps both the helper and the helped.

Biblical Christianity has a better record of helping people connect to great causes than any movement in world history. 90 percent of christian congregations undertake programs of human service and welfare for their communities. More than two-thirds of them maintain programs for international service and health care.[2] After twenty-three years as a Wall Street banker, Jerry Estess quit his job and began working for the Jericho Project, a program to aid the homeless. "I love it," he said when a reporter asked how he liked the change. Not everyone who connects with God feels this kind of call, but everyone has the opportunity to connect with great causes through which life takes on eternal and transcendent dimensions. Through these causes, life becomes more meaningful, blessed, and abundant.

Distortions of Meeting Human Need

Biblical Christianity meets human need in three ways, and we can distort that focus in three ways. If we stop helping people connect with God, we have distorted biblical Christianity. Other kinds of distortion occur when we cease helping people connect with other people or stop helping them connect with great causes. A wall poster in the youth room in a Florida church says, "Life Is What We Are Alive To." We can be alive regardless of what we are alive to. We cannot be *abundantly* alive without connecting with God, people, and great causes.

Making Tracks

A surprise snowstorm caught commuters on the evening local unprepared. No one was wearing overshoes. Groans and moans came from the riders, especially the women, as the train pulled up beside a station platform blanketed with deep snow. The conductor eased the tension by shouting these instructions: "All gentlemen with big feet get off first and make tracks for the ladies!" As each of us looks back over our life, we remember times when people made the path easier for us. Biblical Christianity asks each of us to leave tracks for others.

John Claypool, somewhere in one of his writings, told about Anthony DeMello's anger as he looked at a starving child. DeMello lifted his eyes to heaven and said, "God, how could you allow such suffering? Why don't you do something?"

After a long silence, DeMello was startled to hear the voice of God say to him, "I certainly have done something—I made you." According to biblical Christianity, that is what God says to each of us.

Discovery Questions for Group Study

1. Do you agree or disagree that there are three ways to meet human need—connecting with God, connecting with people, and connecting with great causes?

2. Ask everyone in the group who is willing to share which of the three ways of meeting human need is most important to them personally. Why?

3. In which of the three ways of meeting human need listed in this chapter do you think our denomination is most effective? Our congregation?

4. To which of the three ways of meeting human need listed in this chapter do you think our denomination should give more attention? Our congregation?

CHAPTER 18

GOD'S LIGHTHOUSE

During the 1940s, a storm destroyed a village church on the northern coast of England. The poverty of the members prevented them from immediately rebuilding. After a few months, a British admiral appeared in the village and asked where the pastor lived. When the two of them sat down to talk, the admiral wanted to know whether the church intended to rebuild. When he learned of their financial problems, he said that if they could not rebuild, the British government would need to do it for them. The church spire was a landmark on all the maps of the British Navy. It would be cheaper to rebuild the church than to reprint all the maps.[1]

The Church serves a similar function on the rugged coast of life. It helps us to know where we are, points us toward Christ, and helps us to arrive safely home. This does not mean it is perfect. The Church is a divine institution because its leader is Christ and its objectives are divine. But because each local franchise is managed by people, it always falls short of divinity at the operational level. Sometimes, it falls into disrepair. Sometimes, a storm of controversy blows it down. Yet, in spite of its flaws and the imperfections of its leaders, nothing else in human society can as effectively fulfill its function. *Biblical Christianity is therefore church-centered*. Christians are not just called to be individual disciples. They are called to come together and be the Church.

Why did Jesus say so little about an organization which was to become so crucial in extending his work? The Gospel record reports him telling the disciples only one thing on this subject: He would build his Church on faith like that of Peter and the gates of hell would not prevail against it (Matt. 16:18). Beyond that comment, silence. Why? We are not sure. Perhaps Jesus had modeled the Church with his inner circle of twelve disciples and did not need to discuss it. Perhaps he knew that organizational matters are never as important as vision and conviction. Perhaps he knew that people who enter a new level of consciousness through a faith connection with God will automatically figure out a way to get organized so that others in their generation and the next can have that experience. Perhaps he simply left that task to those who would come later.

Whatever the reason for Jesus' plan, it worked. While the four Gospels are virtually silent regarding the Church, the disciples immediately built it, and the other New Testament writings describe its nature and function. Paul writes the Corinthians, "Now you are the body of Christ and individually members of it" (I Cor. 12:27). Dozens of other verses supplement this basic definition, but they all point in the same directions: Christ is the head of this organization (Col. 1:18); individual disciples of Christ are members of this organization (Eph. 5:30); churches continue the words and work of Jesus by helping people to form and strengthen their personal relationship with God and extend God's loving concern to other people (II Cor. 5:20); the members of this organization meet together, worship together, pray together, study together, proclaim the Good News of Christ together, baptize new members, and help those who are in pain or difficulty (Acts 2:41-47).

The history of the Greek word for church has embedded within it an excellent description of the Church's nature. The ancient Greek word, *ekklesia*, had no religious meaning whatever. It signified a public assembly of the citizens of a town. In Acts 19:39, Luke uses *ekklesia* in exactly that way. The early disciples appropriated that secular word and made it sacred. They used *ekklesia* to signify the individual bodies of Christ and to describe all the churches collectively (Eph. 1:22ff; 3:10; 5:23). *Ekklesia* is thus a marriage of the secular and the sacred. Coming from our individual, secular settings, we connect with Christ and become disciples. Because we are disciples connected to Christ, we connect with each other and become *ekklesia*, the body of Christ—working together to continue saying what he said, doing what he did, and being what he was.

Connected to Christ

Jesus in the stable and on the cross was an incarnation of God's love. The Church, his body, is a continuation of that incarnation.

Churches illustrate their connection to Christ in many ways. In the villages of Switzerland, travelers notice three types of village churches. Most of the villages have churches with clocks on their steeples and bells inside. Some of the smaller village churches have no clocks, only bells. Some of the small churches in the tiniest hamlets perched high on the mountainsides have neither a clock nor a bell. Among the many ministries of the Church, it fulfills those three functions in every age. It calls people to repentance by standing tall and telling the right time. Occasionally, it rings out loud prophetic bells. And sometimes it just stands there, reminding us by its presence in the noisy traffic of important daily affairs that there are matters of even greater importance, which we can hear only through the still, small voice. Yet, a church is not a church because it does these kinds of work. Like the electrical circuit box on a house, a church is a church because of the source to which it is connected. If churches disconnect from Christ, their work becomes something less than church work.

Meeting Together

Jean Peterson wrote a book entitled *You Can't Be Human Alone*. The New Testament says you cannot be a Christian alone. "Do not forsake the assembling of yourselves together," the writer of Hebrews says (Heb. 10:25). The Bible reports no freelance Christianity; it is always corporate. Within those gatherings, amazing power appears. It was while the group was together that Pentecost happened. Again and again, we see happening in the early churches what Jesus had predicted: "Where two or three are gathered in my name, there am I in the midst of them" (Matt. 18:20).

Worshiping Together

Why do Christians worship together? Nothing else can accomplish for us what worship can accomplish. Worship helps us to renew our relationship with God. Worship reprints in our minds the words and work of Christ. Worship provides the opportunity to give thanks for God's forgiveness and continuing presence with us through the Holy Spirit. Worship heals our personal brokenness. Worship empowers us for meaningful, purposeful living that reaches out in love to others.

Several hundred years before the birth of Christ, Plato defined man as a being in search of meaning. Subsequent centuries of evidence confirm that definition. The worshiping community of faith is a chief means of meeting this need. A poll of national church leaders gave a long list of options, asking them to check the items which have the greatest influence in the lives of Christians. Even though many of the respondents were media leaders, worship services were voted the most influential item on the list. These leaders judged radio, TV, and magazines as having minimal influence in people's lives.[2]

Jesus attended public worship each week (Luke 4:16) and was well enough known that he was invited to be a lay reader and preacher. Worship is still a characteristic of persons who wish to retain a strong faith connection with God. A Christian who does not worship is like someone who believes in education but never goes to school.

Giving Christ to New Generations

In one of the many current skirmishes between right-wing Christians and the officials who approve public school textbooks, the pastor of a conservative denomination objected to the manner in which the phrase "the Church" was used in a history of medieval Europe. The textbook's author defended the phrase by saying to that pastor, "But you and I would not be Christians today were it not for the Church in the Middle Ages."

"Ha!" the pastor replied with flashing eyes. "I would."[3]

This observation seems an overly optimistic assessment of reality. Without the Church, the Good News of Christ becomes old news and eventually unknown news.

Distortions of the Church

How do we distort the church-centered nature of biblical Christianity? By deleting any of the four characteristics of *ekklesia*—by not connecting with Christ, not meeting together, not worshiping together, and not giving Christ to new generations. When we stop doing any one of these four, we stop "reincarnating" Christ in our own lives and "re-presenting" Christ to others. When that happens, we stop being the body of Christ and start being just a body.

Out of the Ashes

Ancient Egyptian mythology tells about the phoenix. This bird, as large as an eagle, had scarlet and gold feathers and gave a beautiful cry. Only one phoenix lived at a time, with a very long lifespan. When its death approached, it built a nest of boughs and spices. After setting the nest on fire, the phoenix was consumed in the flames. From the fire and ashes, a new phoenix rose into the air.

The phoenix is a perfect image of the Church. The Church is the body of Christ, capable of rising anew in each generation. Out of the ashes of dysfunctional traditionalism into which religious institutions inevitably fall over a period of time, the Church is always reborn. And like the phoenix, it is always born full grown—capable, through a living community, of "re-presenting" the living Christ to persons who urgently need to enter the kingdom of spiritual reality to which he invites them.

Discovery Questions for Group Study

1. Do you think the imperfections of churches and their leaders have seriously damaged the ability of congregations to communicate Christ to this generation?

2. Ask everyone in the group who feels comfortable in doing so to tell which aspects of church life are the most helpful in communicating Christ to them.

3. In addition to connecting with Christ, meeting together,

worshiping together, and giving Christ to the next generation, do you think churches have other, equally important characteristics?

4. In your opinion, what are the worst ways that churches and their leaders can distort the church-centered nature of biblical Christianity?

5. Which of the four possible distortions of biblical Christianity—not connecting with Christ, not meeting together, not worshiping together, not giving Christ to new generations—do you think are most common in our community? Our denomination?

CHAPTER 19

EDDIE OR THE DRAGON?

An exotic restaurant serving a wealthy clientele was named *Eddie and the Dragon*. A beggar came to the back door one day and said to the woman who appeared to be in charge, "I haven't eaten in days. Could you spare me some food?"

"Get out of here," yelled the woman. "We don't feed beggars."

The man left, but a few minutes later he was back. "What now?" the irritated woman asked.

The beggar, looking up at the sign over the door, *Eddie and the Dragon*, said, "I wonder if I can talk with Eddie this time?"

Two of the strongest contemporary trends in Western culture are opposites. One—the desire to meet human need—is consistent with biblical Christianity. The other—an individualistic separation from other people—is moving thought patterns in a dragon direction. The separation of self from society has been encouraged by countless subtle environmental influences during the past few decades—separate bedrooms for children, individual bathrooms, two cars per family, two careers per marriage, hundreds of options in car models, and individuals working at computer screens instead of with other people. These patterns of individualism that have replaced patterns of close personal relationships have provided many positive changes. One aspect of individuation has, however, been negative: It has increased our inclination to be judgmental and intolerant. As we have less personal connection with each other, we tend to become more like the dragon half of *Eddie and the Dragon*.

This phenomenon of increasing individualism and an associated rise of intolerance has impacted denominations in a strange, unexpected way. The cooperative spirit born at mid-century as a result of World War II began moving the various families of faith to work closer together. Several major denominational mergers resulted from this ecumenical climate. Three of these mergers—the Presbyterians, the Lutherans, and the United Methodists—total more than twenty million people. A less clearly seen trend—individualism—has moved these three and every other individual denomination toward greater internal strife in the latter part of this century. Within each major denomination, one or several splinter groups have appeared. Each is trying to redirect the priorities of its denomination. The fourteen-million-member Southern Baptist Church, torn by the inerrancy struggle, is one example. Similar, though less publicized, rifts are raising internal havoc in all the others. A stranger stopped to ask a teenager where to find a certain church. The boy told him to go one block south. "That is the United Church," he said. "Go one more block south, and you come to a church that is not united. That's it!"[1] Many contemporary denominations fit that description. They are uniting with each other and dividing internally.

Two mental culprits are causing this internal church strife: One is the cultural pressure toward individualism. The other is our failure to take seriously one of the major teachings of biblical Christianity—tolerance. In his parable of the wheat and the weeds, Jesus tells us to leave judgment to God (Matt. 13:24-30). On another occasion, he said, "Judge not, that you be not judged" (Matt. 7:1). In speaking to the crowd ready to execute the woman for adultery, he said, "Let him who is without sin among you be the first to throw a stone at her" (John 8:7). *Biblical Christianity is, therefore, tolerance-centered.* Yet, the organizational life of denominations and their individual congregations is increasingly filled with rock-throwing judgmentalism.

The Only Rational Answer

A woman came into a shoe store and said, "I want to exchange these snake-skin pumps. See these scratches on them."

The diplomatic clerk agreed that the shoes were scratched and brought out another pair. Following a careful examination, the woman said, "These are marred, too."

After another trip to the back room, the clerk came back loaded down with ten boxes. The woman methodically examined each one, then said, "They are all imperfect."

"Madam," the salesman said, now far beyond his usual diplomatic demeanor, "I'm not perfect. You're not perfect. How can you expect a snake to be perfect?" Tolerance is the only rational answer to human imperfection and differences of opinion in congregations. If we expect other people to be perfect, we end up discarding all of them. The only defense against that inclination is to become totally intolerant of intolerance.

Distortions of Tolerance

A news story told about a family whose church denied them the privilege of burying their son in the church cemetery because they were inactive members. Another news report told of a Scottish church that suspended one of its elders because he had attended Catholic funeral services. Finding a balance between maintaining high standards in a church and living out Jesus' injunction to love one another is never simple. It seems clear, however, that in the present days we need to less often ask the question, "What is the rule?" and more often ask the question, "Is this love?" Tolerance without conviction is not a virtue, but intolerance without love leads to far greater sin.

An old Hindu story tells about a middle-aged man who returned from the river with a large basket on his shoulder. He met his son, who inquired where he had been. The father told the son, "Your grandfather was no longer able to work in any way. All he did was eat and sleep. So, I took him to the river in a basket and dumped him in."

The boy thought a moment and said to his father, "Save the basket." When religious people decide to make rules and regulations more important than love, they set up a climate in which everyone is saving baskets for each other.

The Worst Word

It is reported that someone once asked Carl Sandburg to name the worst word in the English language. "Exclusive," he said. His answer was biblical. Exclusive is another way of saying intolerant. It cuts people out. Intolerance is not just an unbiblical trait for church leaders; it is also impractical. Gallup poll research identifies "narrow religious beliefs" as one of the reasons cited by people who stay away from church attendance.[2] Many Christians have in recent years highly criticized the sin of excluding blacks and females from churches and leadership roles. Perhaps it is time to highlight the sin of theological exclusiveness, too—since both liberals and conserV-atives seem equally guilty of it.

Gandhi once said that if we are to make progress, we must stop repeating history and make new history. The time seems right for making some new history in regard to our differing viewpoints about the Christian faith. How can this happen? How can we have both high standards and loving tolerance? There is only one answer: By urging other Christians to do with all their heart and energy what God has called them to do and gifted them for doing—helping to lift the burdens and heal the hurts of humanity. Trying to force other Christians into agreeing with our viewpoints is usually a fruitless waste of energy that drives us apart. Trying to love and respect the unique gifts God has given other Christians moves us toward peace and unity. That is precisely what happened at the Jerusalem Council reported in the Book of Acts. Peter had a gift for working with the Jews. Paul had a gift for working with the Gentiles. They agreed to use those gifts and refuse to abuse each other for using them. One word for that behavior is *tolerance*. Another word is *love*.

In an old churchyard near Dumfries, Scotland, stands a monument to John Craik, a schoolteacher. He was the writing master in the famous Dumfries Academy more than 120 years ago. An old man who had been a student there said that Craik had extraordinary skill in teaching people without making them feel inadequate. Whenever a student made an inkblot on his or her writing book, John Craik did not scold. He sat down beside the youngster and carefully used his pen to shape the inkblot into the form of an angel.[3] This present era is an especially good time for Christians to turn the inkblots of disagreement from the past into angels of tolerance.

Discovery Questions for Group Study

1. Do you agree or disagree with the observation that denominations are working closer together but have more internal strife?

2. Ask group members to give examples of ways that religious intolerance hurts people in our society.

3. In addition to the inclination toward perfectionistic judgmentalism, are there other reasons why Christians exhibit intolerance toward each other?

4. Do you think the recommendation to concentrate on love rather than rules is an oversimplification of the problem Christians face in trying to maintain high standards? Why?

5. Can you think of ways that intolerance has violated love in our denomination? How would you suggest that these problems be improved?

CHAPTER 20

DANGEROUS FREEDOM

Nature seems to love variety. Insect experts have identified 2,500 species of flies.

Religious statisticians say there are 20,800 Christian denominations in the world and estimate that this number will keep growing. How should Christians feel about this trend? Is it negative or positive? Jesus seems to agree with nature. When the disciples complain that a stranger is using his name to heal people, Jesus replies, "He that is not against us is for us" (Mark 10:40). On another occasion he told them, "And I have other sheep, that are not of this fold" (John 10:16). The Apostle Paul seems to say the same: He rejoices that Christ is proclaimed, even in diversity (Phil. 1:17-18). Paul Minear, a highly respected biblical scholar, says that New Testament authors used ninety-six models to describe the early Church.[1] The Bible's format, with its four different life of Christ stories in the four Gospels, seems to substantiate this freedom and diversity attitude. *Surely, therefore, biblical Christianity is freedom-centered.*

Yet, how can this freedom theory stand up to the scrutiny of logical analysis? Truth is in some ways very narrow. Not all roads lead home. Sailors use a compass because not all directions are equally beneficial. On a final exam, the various answer possibilities are seldom of equal value. Do we have the freedom to believe anything that comes to mind and call it Christian thinking?

Where do we draw the line between the freedom of thought the Bible advocates and the distortions of truth that arise when people bend biblical beliefs beyond a recognizable shape? Historical evidence provides ammunition for arguing in both directions—toward extreme freedom and toward extreme conformity. On one hand, the Church of Jesus Christ is quite obviously a spiritual entity, larger than any individual congregation, denomination, or institutional structure. Therefore, if we live out Jesus' command to love one another, granting our religious neighbors freedom of thought on doctrinal matters is our only option. On the other hand, the freedom to believe anything leads eventually to the freedom to believe nothing. This moves us outside the circle of authentic biblical Christianity.

Distortions of Freedom

In trying to resolve their dilemma regarding how much freedom to allow in freedom of thought, Christians face two opposite dangers—conviction without freedom and freedom without conviction.

Conviction Without Freedom. Much of Christian history is a story of warring armies fighting over who is right with all sides determined to take no prisoners. The locals in Charleston, South Carolina, have a saying that at the point where the Ashley River and the Cooper River come together at Charleston, they form the Atlantic Ocean. That tongue-in-cheek viewpoint requires the same kind of bias we have seen in the avid and destructive denominationalism of past centuries. Many Christians have assumed that the sea of true Christianity is formed at the point where their personal opinions and Jesus Christ come together. This makes for aggressive evangelistic fervor but tends to produce behavior inconsistent with serving the Prince of Peace. During the 1971 Irish religious riots in Belfast, a cartoon caption said, "Watch your language around Pat. He's very religious." Pat is pictured holding a tommy gun and looking across a street strewn with heaps of rubble and several bodies.

Freedom Without Conviction. In 1924, 6 percent of American mothers said tolerance was an important virtue to instill in their children; today, 47 percent of mothers feel that way. In 1924, 50 percent of mothers said loyalty to the church was important, while today only 22 percent say that.[2] This major shift of attitude has shoved many Christians in a new direction. Their greatest contemporary danger seems the opposite of the Christian antagonisms so prevalent in the past. The virtue of Christian openness and tolerance has made the minds of many a rubbish can that discriminates against nothing and collects everything. Such minds become totally unproductive in communicating biblical Christianity to others. Capable of believing everything, they lack clarity and conviction about anything. This kind of thinking produces a false ecumenism that disagrees with very little because it believes very little.

The concept of "pluralism," a contemporary word used to describe Christian openness to the ideas of others, is a virtue unless it becomes empty-headedness. Phrases like "everything is relative," "live and let live," and "go with the flow" are not Christian virtues if they replace a belief in truth, good, and loving behavior. John Wesley believed in a "catholic spirit" of tolerance, but he also said that some beliefs are so essential that they define the boundary between Christians and non-Christians.[3] White lines in the middle of the highway limit your freedom, but they also keep you from crashing into other cars. When we begin to think Christian freedom has no limits, we fall into the sin of saying that the core beliefs of Christianity—God, Jesus Christ, and the Holy Spirit—do not matter.

Ironically, the extreme freedom of thought recommended by many advocates of Christian unity among denominations has within it seeds of disunity. If pure individual interpretation of the Bible replaces the accumulated wisdom of the centuries regarding what scripture texts mean, the soil in which unity can grow washes away. Genuine Christian unity, while it is always based on freedom of thought, is always held together at the center by some kind of *content* focus.

Freedom with Conviction

Freedom without conviction becomes a mental sieve that takes in everything and holds on to nothing. Conviction without freedom becomes a crazy federal mint manager who tries to pour all the hot metal into the same mold, refusing to affirm the value of different types of coins. How can we avoid these opposite extremes? In four ways:

By focusing on Christ. The fundamental basis of Jesus' teaching was the presence among us of a supernatural being whose power transcends the normal cause and effect laws of nature that we can see with our five senses. "God is here among us," Jesus was saying. He lived his life in a faith relationship with that invisible other and urged those around him to do the same. Jesus both taught and was the *content*, or *Word*, of this God-person relationship possibility with which he suggested everyone should connect. When we focus our minds on Christ, we are focusing on the hub of biblical Christianity.

By focusing on freedom in Christ. Christian love demands that we let people think for themselves and develop their faith relationship with God through their own reason, their own understanding of the Bible, their own prayer, and their own experience with spiritual reality.

By focusing on conviction about Christ. Granting others freedom does not mean we must stifle our own beliefs. We can love, respect, and dialogue with persons of other denominations and world religions while boldly proclaiming that Jesus is Lord.

By focusing on the love Christ taught. To love Christ means to believe he is the answer for all our neighbors. To love our neighbors means that we grant them the freedom to believe or not to believe this. Christian conviction does not call us to make judgments about the destiny of other human beings—to say they are goats on their way to hell and we are sheep on the way to heaven. Yes, the Bible says that Jesus is the only Savior: "No one comes to the Father, but by me" (John 14:6). But the Bible also says, "Love one another as I have loved you" (John 15:12). The biblical Christian has deep conviction, but love prevents that conviction from hardening into judgments that deny the freedom of conviction to others.

Getting the Grain to Market

Granting others freedom of thought is a characteristic of persons who believe in biblical Christianity. Freedom of thought is not, however, the central goal of biblical Christianity. The central goal is to help people come into a faith relationship with God and grow in that relationship. When Christians neglect that central goal in favor of "letting everyone do their own thing," they are committing sin (focusing the mind on a goal other than on God). Our role is not to persecute those who think differently than we do (as has often been the case with many intolerant Christians). Nor is our role to disregard those who think differently from us (as is the case with those who advocate a ecumenism without conviction, which says all world religions are equal). Our role is to tell the good news of Jesus Christ—that God loves us and wants us to connect with him in a personal faith relationship that makes all things new in our personal life and our world.

A visiting evangelist stopped by to see an old farmer. "Harry," the preacher said, "What denomination do you belong to?"

Harry replied that when his grain was ready to sell, it did not matter whether he took it to town by the gravel road, the dirt road, or the highway. He said that the buyer never asked him which road he took to town. He only asked whether the grain was good. "So, I don't think it much matters what denomination I belong to," Harry said, "I believe in freedom of thought. I do not want to be hemmed in by doctrine."

"I totally agree," said the evangelist. "But let me ask you this: What happens if you believe in freedom so much that you do not get around to taking your grain to town by any road?"

The freedom advocated in biblical Christianity can be dangerous—if we substitute discussing roads for taking a road.

Discovery Questions for Group Study

1. Do you think the willingness to grant people freedom of thought in denominational preference has increased in recent decades?

2. Can you cite instances where freedom of thought regarding Christianity is still quite restricted?

3. List the positive reasons why freedom of thought in religious matters is essential.

4. List any negatives you can think of regarding freedom of thought as it relates to the Christian faith.

5. Which of the two distortions noted in this chapter—conviction without freedom and freedom without conviction—do you think is most prevalent in our denomination?

NOTES

Introduction

1. Joe Hale, address at 1986 World Methodist Conference from "United Methodist Conference," *United Methodist Reporter*, August 1, 1986.

1. Slivers and Substitutes

1. Jack O'Brian, syndicated newspaper column, November 21, 1970.

2. The Perfect Copy

1. Surah 4:171 (*Koran*).
2. B. Clayton Bell, "The Focal Point of Faith," *Preaching* (January-February 1987): p. 12.
3. Beth Pratt, "A Child's Reflections not to be Taken Lightly," *Lubbock Avalanche Journal* Sunday, May 25, 1986, sec. E-7.
4. Alan Walker, *Standing Up to Preach* (Nashville: Discipleship Resources, 1983), p. 44.
5. Eric W. Hayden, *Searchlight on Spurgeon* (Princeton, N.J.: Pilgrim Press, 1973), p. 234.
6. David Branon, *Our Daily Bread*, vol. 29, nos. 2-3 (May-June 1984).

3. God's Microwave

1. John F. MacArthur, Jr., *The Charismatics: A Doctrinal Perspective* (Grand Rapids: Lamplighter Books, 1978), p. 28.
2. Richard P. Heitzenrater, "Practical Theologian," *The Elusive Mr. Wesley*, vol. 1 (Nashville: Abingdon Press, 1984), p. 153.

4. God's Magnetic Force Field

1. "Many Place Human Reason Ahead of God to Solve Life's Problems," *Emerging Trends*, vol. 9, no. 6 (June 1987).

2. "Teen Belief in Witchcraft Is on the Rise," *Emerging Trends*, vol. 11, no. 1 (January 1989).

3. J. Peter Pelkonen, "Preaching through the Year," *The Clergy Journal* (May-June 1986): p. 16.

5. Window, Mirror, and Picture

1. *Institutes*, IV, viii, 8 FF; I, vi, 2; quoted in "Bible Literacy and the Inner Life," *Bible Literacy Today* (Fall, 1988): p. 42.

2. *Sammatliche Schriften*, 3, 21; quoted in "Bible Literacy and the Inner Life," p. 44.

3. Richard P. Heitzenrater, *The Elusive Mr. Wesley*, vol. 1 (Nashville: Abingdon Press, 1984), p. 152.

4. Jonathon Kozol, "Why Do Illiterate People Want to Read?" *Global Sermon Notes*, No. 87-7 (September, 1987).

5. *The National Christian Reporter*, editorial (December 31, 1982): p. 2.

6. Murray W. Downey, *The Art of Soul-Winning*, 2nd ed. (Grand Rapids: Baker Book House, 1989), p. 175.

6. Aiming Our Satellite Dish

1. *National & International Religion Report* (January 30, 1989): p. 8.

2. Extracts from "The Shape of Major Trends: A Resource and Response Paper for National Ministries Long-Range Planning—Looking Toward the Year 2000" and "Additional Trends" compiled by Richard M. Jones. Presented at the 1987 Evangelism Convocation for the American Baptist Churches, St. Louis, Missouri.

3. Leslie Conrad, "Preaching through the Year," *The Clergy Journal*, vol. 64, no. 7 (May-June 1988): p. 81.

4. *Pulpit Helps*, vol. 10, no. 3 (December 1984): p. 14.

7. Let's Be Reasonable

1. Richard Gilmour, *Bible History* (New York: Benziger Brothers, 1936), p. 299.

2. Alvin Jackson, Sermon at a dedication service for Ray of Hope Christian Church, Atlanta, Georgia, June 28, 1988.

8. Enlarging Our Currency

1. Frederick C. Gill, *Through the Year with Wesley* (Nashville: The Upper Room, 1983), p. 182.

2. Willmar Thorkelson, "Tough Targets," *The National Christian Reporter* (January 16, 1987): p. 3.

9. In Good Company

1. S.H. Simmons, *How to Be the Life of the Podium* (New York: AMACON, 1982), pp. 110-11.

11. God's Security System

1. Herbert Vander Lugt, "The Peace-filled Life," *Our Daily Bread*, vol. 29, nos. 6-7 (September-October 1984).
2. Paul R. Van Gorder, "Breakfast from God," *Our Daily Bread*, vol. 33, nos. 3, 4, 5 (June, July, August 1988).
3. Henry G. Bosch, "Be a Pine Tree," *Our Daily Bread*, vol. 33, nos. 9, 10, 11 (December, January, February 1988-89).
4. *Chicago Tribune*, as reported by Martin E. Marty in *Context* (June 15, 1987).
5. "For Safety's Sake," *Pulpit Helps*, vol. 14, no. 2 (November 1988).
6. Paul R. Van Gorder, "Who Saved the Robins," *Our Daily Bread*, vol. 32, no. 12; vol. 33, nos. 1, 2 (March, April, May 1988).

12. Cure for Future Tense

1. R. E. Allen, "Commitments Sought Require Commitments Kept," *Executive Speeches*, vol. 3, no. 3 (October 1988).
2. Martin E.P. Seligman, "Submissive Death: Giving Up on Life," *Psychology Today*, vol. 7 (May 1974): p. 83.
3. Martin R. De Haan II, "Live Options," *Our Daily Bread*, vol. 33, nos. 6, 7, 8 (September, October, November 1988).
4. Colbert S. Cartwright, *Clergy Talk*, vol. 10, no. 1 (January 1989): p. 3.
5. A sermon by Joe Harding at Central United Protestant Church, Richland, Washington, November 10, 1985.
6. John Naisbitt "Booming Business of Comedy Gives Rise to War of Wits," *Trendletter* (March 30, 1989): p. 6.

13. Better Than Happiness

1. "Hebrews/Lesson 7," *1988 Community Bible Study* (Falls Church, Va.: Community Bible Study, 1988), p. 8.

14. Discipleship

1. Leslie B. Flynn, *The Twelve* (Wheaton, Ill.: Victor Books, 1986), p. 41.
2. *Emerging Trends*, vol. 10, no. 7 (September 1988): p. 2.

3. *The Good News Link*, vol 13, no. 1 (Spring 1989): p. 2.
4. Richard P. Heitzenrater, *The Elusive Mr. Wesley*, vol. 1 (Nashville: Abingdon Press, 1984), p. 151.
5. Martin R. De Haan II, "Spectator Risks," *Our Daily Bread*, vol. 33, nos. 6, 7, 8 (September, October, November 1988).
6. Bonaro Overstreet, *Understanding Fear* (New York: Harper & Row, 1951).
7. Leslie B. Flynn, *The Twelve*, p. 126.
8. *First Christian Church Newsletter*, Spearman, Tex. (November 14, 1983).

15. What God Looks Like

1. Bart Starr, in *The Christian Athlete*.
2. R. Southey, *Life of Wesley* (London: Oxford University Press, 1925), p. 359.
3. Ian McCrae, ed., *Global Sermon Notes*, no. 88-02 (February 1988).

16. Love in Work Clothes

1. William Carols Williams, "Asphodel, That Greeny Flower," *Collected Poems 1939—1962*, (New York: New Directions, 1969), p. 3.
2. Stephen King, "Everything You Need to Know About Writing Successfully—in Ten Minutes," *The Writer*, vol. 99, no. 7 (July 1986): p. 10.
3. Dag Hammarskjöld, "1956," *Markings*, trans. Leif Sjöberg and W. H. Auden (New York: Alfred A. Knopf, 1964).
4. William Blake, "To the Deists," *Jerusalem* in *Selected Poetry of William Blake*, Northrop Frye, ed. (New York: Random House, 1953), p. 289.
5. William G. Chrystal, *The Fellowship of Prayer* (St. Louis, Mo.: CBP Press, 1987), March 23 reading.

17. The Heart of What Matters

1. George Gallup, Jr., ed., "Religion in America" *Emerging Trends* (March 1986).
2. *The National Christian Reporter*, vol. 8, no. 43 (December 23, 1988).

18. God's Lighthouse

1. Jesse M. Bader, *Evangelism in a Changing America* (St. Louis, Mo.: Bethany Press, 1957), p. 68.
2. "Evangelical Leaders Poll: Part II," *Evangelical Newsletter* (January 18, 1985), p. 4.

3. Raymond English, *National Review* (April 15, 1989) as quoted by Martin Marty in *Context*, vol. 21, no. 8.

19. Eddie or the Dragon?

1. Leslie B. Flynn, *When the Saints Come Storming In* (Wheaton, Ill.: Victor Books, 1988), p. 16.
2. The Gallup Organization, *The Unchurched American* (Princeton N.J.: The Princeton Religion Research Center, 1978).
3. David A. MacLennan, "Priming the Preacher's Pump," *Church Management* (August 1966): p. 17.

20. Dangerous Freedom

1. Paul S. Minear, *Image of the Church in the New Testament* (Philadelphia: The Westminster Press, 1960).
2. "Demo Memo," *American Demographics* (December 1988): p. 10.
3. "Book Raps 'Theological Pluralism' Statement," *Lubbock Avalanche Journal* (January 10, 1987).